THE AUSTRALIAN
Women's Weekly
sweet things

fruit tarts • café cakes • petit fours • biscuits • desserts

CONTENTS

The oven temperatures in this book are for conventional ovens; if you have a fan-forced oven, decrease the temperature by 10-20 degrees. A measurement conversion chart appears on the back flap of this book.

FRUIT TARTS & CAKES

raspberry and lychee tarts

PREP + COOK TIME 1 HOUR (+ REFRIGERATION) | MAKES 8

You will need about 3 punnets of raspberries for this recipe.

300g (9½ ounces) lychees

450g (14½ ounces) raspberries

PASTRY

1¾ cups (260g) plain (all-purpose) flour

125g (4 ounces) cold unsalted butter, chopped

½ cup (110g) raw sugar

1 egg, beaten lightly

VANILLA CUSTARD

2 cups (500ml) milk

1 vanilla bean

4 egg yolks

½ cup (110g) caster (superfine) sugar

1 tablespoon cornflour (cornstarch)

1 Make pastry.
2 Grease eight 10cm (4-inch) round loose-based fluted flan pans. Divide pastry into 8 portions. Roll each portion between sheets of baking paper until large enough to line pans. Lift pastry into pans, press into base and sides; trim excess pastry.

Prick base all over with a fork. Cover; refrigerate 30 minutes.
3 Preheat oven to 180°C/350°F.
4 Place pans on an oven tray. Bake pastry cases about 20 minutes or until browned lightly. Cool.
5 Meanwhile, make vanilla custard.
6 Peel, halve and seed lychees. Spoon custard into pastry cases; top with lychees and raspberries. Dust with icing sugar, if you like.

PASTRY Sift flour into large bowl; rub in butter with fingertips until mixture is crumbly. Stir in sugar, then egg until ingredients just come together. Knead dough on lightly floured surface until smooth. Flatten dough slightly, wrap in plastic wrap; refrigerate 20 minutes.

VANILLA CUSTARD Place milk in medium saucepan. Split vanilla bean in half lengthways; scrape seeds into pan. Bring milk to the boil. Meanwhile, whisk egg yolks, sugar and cornflour in medium heatproof bowl until combined. Whisk hot milk mixture into egg mixture; return custard to pan. Cook, stirring, over low heat, until mixture boils and thickens. Transfer custard to medium bowl, cover surface with plastic wrap; refrigerate 1 hour.

plum tart

PREP + COOK TIME 45 MINUTES | SERVES 4

4 red-fleshed plums (450g), halved, seeds removed

1 sheet puff pastry

2 tablespoons ground almonds

1 tablespoon caster (superfine) sugar

1 tablespoon plum jam

1 teaspoon water

1 Preheat oven to 240°C/475°F. Line oven tray with baking paper.

2 Cut plum halves into eighths.

3 Halve pastry sheet; place on tray. Lightly score a 1cm border around sides of pastry; prick inside edges with fork.

4 Sprinkle ground almonds and half the sugar over pastry (do not sprinkle over border). Arrange plums, cut-side down on pastry; sprinkle with remaining sugar.

5 Bake tart 25 minutes or until pastry is puffed and golden, and plums are beginning to brown. Combine jam with the water in a small bowl until smooth; brush over pastry edges. Serve tarts warm.

tip These tarts are best eaten hot or warm. The ground almonds are used to mop up all the plum juices to avoid the pastry becoming soggy. You could use other types of ground nuts, if you like.

nectarine and raspberry clafoutis

PREP + COOK TIME 1 HOUR | SERVES 6

500g (1 pound) yellow nectarines, halved, seeds removed

60g (2 ounces) butter, softened

½ cup (110g) caster (superfine) sugar

4 eggs

½ cup (60g) ground almonds

300ml (½ pint) pouring cream

200g (6½ ounces) raspberries

1 Preheat oven to 180°C/350°F.

2 Cut nectarines into wedges. Divide between six ¾-up (180ml) shallow ovenproof dishes.

3 Beat butter and sugar in a large bowl with an electric mixer until light and fluffy. Whisk in eggs, one at a time, then whisk in ground almonds and cream until just combined. Pour batter over fruit; scatter with raspberries.

4 Bake clafoutis about 40 minutes or until golden and a knife inserted in the centre comes out clean.

5 Serve clafoutis warm or at room temperature, dusted with a little sifted icing sugar, if you like.

tips Choose freestone nectarines as, when cut, the flesh comes cleanly away from the seeds.

nectarine and almond tart

PREP + COOK TIME 1¾ HOURS (+ REFRIGERATION & COOLING) | SERVES 10

1⅓ cups (200g) plain (all-purpose) flour

125g (4 ounces) cold unsalted butter, chopped

2 tablespoons iced water, approximately

450g (14½ ounces) yellow nectarines

2 tablespoons flaked almonds

ALMOND FRANGIPANE

120g (4 ounces) unsalted butter, softened

½ cup (110g) caster (superfine) sugar

2 eggs

2 tablespoons plain (all-purpose) flour

1 cup (120g) ground almonds

1 Sift flour into a large bowl; rub in butter with fingertips until mixture resembles coarse breadcrumbs. Mix in enough of the water to make ingredients just come together. Knead dough on lightly floured surface until smooth. Flatten dough slightly, wrap in plastic wrap; refrigerate 20 minutes.

2 Grease 20cm (8-inch) round loose-based fluted flan pan. Roll pastry on lightly floured surface, or between sheets of baking paper, until large enough to line pan.

3 Lift pastry into pan; press over base and side, trim excess pastry. Prick base all over with fork; refrigerate 20 minutes.

4 Preheat oven to 200°C/400°F.

5 Place flan pan on oven tray, line pastry with baking paper; fill with dried beans or rice. Bake 15 minutes; remove paper and beans. Bake a further 15 minutes or until pastry is browned lightly and crisp.

6 Meanwhile make almond frangipane.

7 Cut nectarines in half; remove seeds. Cut nectarines into wedges.

8 Spoon frangipane into tart shell; top with nectarines, cut-side up, pushing lightly into frangipane, sprinkle over almonds. Bake about 45 minutes or until golden; cool tart in pan.

ALMOND FRANGIPANE Beat butter and sugar in a medium bowl with an electric mixer until light and fluffy. Beat in eggs, one at a time, until combined. Stir in sifted flour and almonds.

poached plum and ginger sour cream cake

PREP + COOK TIME 1½ HOURS | SERVES 8

125g (4 ounces) butter, softened

1 cup (220g) firmly packed light brown sugar

3 eggs

⅓ cup (80g) sour cream

1 cup (150g) plain (all-purpose) flour

¼ cup (35g) self-raising flour

2 teaspoons ground ginger

¼ teaspoon ground clove

1 tablespoon demerara sugar

POACHED PLUMS

1 cup (220g) caster (superfine) sugar

2 cups (500ml) dry red wine

2 cups (500ml) water

1 cinnamon stick

2 star anise

3 red-fleshed plums (450g), halved, seeds removed

1 Make poached plums.

2 Preheat oven to 170°C/340°F. Grease deep 20cm (8-inch) ring pan.

3 Beat butter and brown sugar in a medium bowl with an electric mixer until light and fluffy. Beat in eggs, one at a time, until combined. Stir in sour cream and sifted flours and spices. Spread mixture into pan. Bake 15 minutes.

4 Working quickly, remove pan from oven; arrange plums on top of cake, cut-side up. Sprinkle with demerara sugar. Bake about a further 50 minutes. Stand cake in pan 5 minutes before turning, top-side up, onto wire rack to cool.

5 Meanwhile, bring reserved syrup to the boil. Boil, uncovered, about 20 minutes or until syrup is reduced by half and has thickened slightly; remove cinnamon stick and star anise.

6 To serve, drizzle warm cake with warm syrup.

POACHED PLUMS Stir sugar, wine, the water, cinnamon and star anise in a medium saucepan over medium-high heat, without boiling, until sugar dissolves; bring to the boil. Add plums, reduce heat; simmer, uncovered, about 5 minutes or until plums are just tender. Remove plums from syrup; cool. Reserve syrup in pan.

serving idea Serve warm with a dollop of double (thick) cream.

chocolate cherry cupcakes

PREP + COOK TIME 1 HOUR (+ REFRIGERATION) | MAKES 20

90g (3 ounces) dark (semi-sweet) chocolate

2 tablespoons cocoa powder

¾ cup (180ml) boiling water

125g (4 ounces) unsalted butter, softened

2 eggs

1 cup (220g) firmly packed dark brown sugar

½ teaspoon vanilla extract

⅓ cup (80g) sour cream

¾ cup (110g) plain (all-purpose) flour

½ cup (75g) self-raising flour

½ teaspoon bicarbonate of soda (baking soda)

⅓ cup (50g) finely chopped dried cherries

50g (1½ ounces) dark (semi-sweet) chocolate, extra

12 fresh cherries (75g)

CHOCOLATE CHERRY GANACHE

270g (8½ ounces) dark (semi-sweet) chocolate

2 tablespoons pouring cream

¼ cup (60ml) cherry liqueur

1 Preheat oven to 170°C/340°F. Line 20 holes of two 12-hole (⅓-cup/80ml) muffin pans with paper cases.

2 Break chocolate into a small saucepan, add cocoa powder and the water; stir over low heat until smooth. Transfer mixture to a large bowl of an electric mixer; cool 10 minutes.

3 Add butter, eggs, sugar, extract, sour cream and sifted flours and soda to the chocolate mixture. Beat with an electric mixer, on low speed, until combined. Increase speed to medium; beat about 2 minutes or until mixture is smooth and changed to a paler colour. Stir in dried cherries.

4 Divide mixture evenly into paper cases. Bake about 20 minutes. Stand cupcakes in pan 5 minutes before turning, top-side up, onto wire rack to cool.

5 Meanwhile, make chocolate cherry ganache.

6 Spoon ganache into piping bag fitted with a 2cm (¾-inch) fluted tube; pipe ganache over cupcakes. Grate extra chocolate, sprinkle over cakes; top with fresh cherries.

CHOCOLATE CHERRY GANACHE Break chocolate into a medium heatproof bowl, add cream and liqueur; stir over a medium saucepan of simmering water until smooth (don't let water touch base of bowl). Remove from heat. Refrigerate about 1 hour or until thick. Beat with electric mixer until smooth.

13

apple tart

PREP + COOK TIME 1¾ HOURS (+ REFRIGERATION) | SERVES 6

1 sheet butter puff pastry

4 medium red-skinned apples (450g)

1 tablespoon caster (superfine) sugar

1 tablespoon lemon juice

1 tablespoon apricot jam

1 tablespoon water

CRÈME PÂTISSIÈRE

2 cups (500ml) milk

1 teaspoon vanilla bean paste

4 egg yolks

⅓ cup (75g) caster (superfine) sugar

¼ cup (35g) cornflour (cornstarch)

15g (½ ounce) butter, softened

1 Make crème pâtissière.

2 Roll pastry between sheets of baking paper until large enough to line a greased 22cm (9-inch) square loose-based fluted flan pan. Lift pastry into pan, press into base and sides; trim excess pastry. Prick base all over with a fork. Cover; refrigerate 20 minutes.

3 Preheat oven to 180°C/350°F.

4 Core and halve apples; slice thinly. Combine apple, sugar and juice in a medium bowl. Spread crème pâtissière into pastry case. Arrange apple slices in slightly overlapping rows, over crème pâtissière. Drizzle with any juices. Bake about 40 minutes or until pastry and apples are golden.

5 Combine jam and the water in a small saucepan. Bring to the boil, stirring constantly, until smooth. Brush mixture over top of apple. Cool; refrigerate about 1 hour before cutting and serving. Dust with a little sifted icing sugar, if you like.

CRÈME PÂTISSIÈRE Heat milk and vanilla bean paste in a medium saucepan, over medium heat, until almost boiling. Meanwhile, whisk egg yolks, sugar and cornflour together in a medium heatproof bowl; gradually whisk in hot milk. Return mixture to pan; whisk over low heat about 5 minutes or until thickened. Remove from heat; stir in butter. Cover surface with plastic wrap; refrigerate crème pâtissière until firm.

A light lemon butter cake filled with a luscious velvety, tartish-sweet lemon curd, drizzled with lemon syrup and covered with a creamy light-as-air fluffy frosting – this cake is a lemon-lover's delight.

lemon curd cake (recipe page 18)

lemon curd cake

PREP + COOK TIME 2 HOURS (+ COOLING) | SERVES 12

250g (8 ounces) butter, softened

2 cups (440g) caster (superfine) sugar

4 eggs

2 cups (300g) self-raising flour

1 cup (150g) plain (all-purpose) flour

200g (6½ ounces) crème fraîche

2 tablespoons lemon juice

LEMON CURD

4 eggs

4 egg yolks

1½ cups (330g) caster (superfine) sugar

150g (4½ ounces) cold unsalted butter

2 tablespoons finely grated lemon rind

⅔ cup (160ml) lemon juice

LEMON SYRUP

⅓ cup (80ml) water

⅓ cup (75g) caster (superfine) sugar

2 tablespoons limoncello liqueur

FLUFFY FROSTING

1 cup (220g) caster (superfine) sugar

⅓ cup (80ml) water

2 egg whites

(pictured on pages 16-17)

1 Make lemon curd and lemon syrup.

2 Preheat oven to 180°C/350°F. Grease two deep 22cm (9-inch) round cake pans; line bases and sides with baking paper.

3 Beat butter and sugar in a large bowl with an electric mixer until light and fluffy. Beat in eggs, one at a time until combined. Stir in sifted flours, crème fraîche and juice, in two batches.

4 Divide mixture evenly between pans; smooth surface. Bake about 35 minutes. Stand cakes in pans 5 minutes before turning, top-side up, onto wire racks to cool.

5 Using a serrated knife, trim tops of cakes so they are level. Split each cake into three layers. Place one layer on a serving plate; brush with a little of the syrup and spread with ½ cup lemon curd. Repeat layering with remaining cake layers, syrup and curd, finishing with a cake layer.

6 Make fluffy frosting. Spread fluffy frosting over top and sides of cake.

LEMON CURD Whisk eggs, egg yolks and sugar in a medium saucepan until smooth. Chop butter into small cubes; add butter, rind and juice to pan. Whisk over low heat until curd thickens. Remove from heat; strain into a medium bowl. Cover surface with plastic wrap; cool.

LEMON SYRUP Stir sugar and the water in a small saucepan over medium heat, without boiling, until sugar dissolves. Bring to the boil; boil, uncovered, without stirring, about 3 minutes or until syrup is thickened. Remove from heat; stir in liqueur. Cool.

FLUFFY FROSTING Combine sugar and the water in a small saucepan; stir with a wooden spoon over high heat, without boiling, until sugar dissolves. Bring to the boil; boil, uncovered, without stirring, about 5 minutes or until the syrup thickens slightly and reaches 114°C/240°F on a sugar thermometer (this is known as 'soft ball stage'). While the syrup is boiling (after about 4 minutes), beat the egg whites in a small bowl with an electric mixer until stiff; keep beating until the syrup reaches the correct temperature. When the syrup is ready, allow the bubbles to subside then pour a very thin stream into the egg whites with mixer operating on medium speed. Continue beating and adding syrup until all the syrup is used. Continue to beat until the frosting stands in stiff peaks, about 10 minutes (frosting should be barely warm).

tips If you don't have a sugar thermometer when making the fluffy frosting, you can test whether the sugar has reached the correct temperature by dropping a teaspoon of the mixture into a glass of cold water – the sugar will form a clear-coloured soft, flexible ball. Remove the sugar ball from the water and press it gently between your thumb and finger and it should flatten easily. You may have to do this test a few times until the soft ball stage is reached. The fluffy frosting should be used immediately, as it sets quite quickly as it cools down and will lose its glossiness. Limoncello is made from the peel only of fragrant lemons. The peel is soaked in a good-quality clear alcohol then diluted with sugar and water.

raspberry, hazelnut and chocolate tart

PREP + COOK TIME 1 HOUR (+ REFRIGERATION & COOLING) | SERVES 18

300g (9½ ounces) frozen raspberries

1 cup (220g) caster (superfine) sugar

1 tablespoon orange juice

270g (8½ ounces) dark (semi-sweet) chocolate, chopped coarsely

25g (¾ ounce) butter

⅔ cup (160ml) pouring cream

¼ cup (60ml) hazelnut-flavoured liqueur

100g (3-ounce) block dark (semi-sweet) chocolate, extra

125g (4 ounces) fresh raspberries

HAZELNUT PASTRY

⅓ cup (45g) roasted hazelnuts

1 cup (150g) plain (all-purpose) flour

⅓ cup (55g) icing (confectioners') sugar

90g (3 ounces) cold unsalted butter, chopped coarsely

1 egg yolk

2 teaspoons iced water, approximately

1 Make hazelnut pastry.

2 Grease 24cm (9½-inch) round loose-based fluted flan pan. Roll pastry between sheets of baking paper until large enough to line flan pan. Lift pastry into pan, press into base and side; trim excess pastry. Prick base all over with a fork. Refrigerate 30 minutes.

3 Preheat oven to 180°C/350°F.

4 Place pan on an oven tray; line pastry with baking paper, fill with dried beans or rice. Bake 15 minutes. Remove paper and beans; bake a further 15 minutes or until browned lightly. Cool.

5 Meanwhile, combine frozen raspberries, sugar and juice in a small saucepan; stir over medium heat, without boiling, until sugar dissolves. Bring to the boil. Reduce heat; simmer, uncovered, stirring occasionally, about 25 minutes or until thick. Cool. Spread cold berry mixture into pastry case.

6 Place chocolate, butter, cream and liqueur into a medium heatproof bowl; stir over a medium saucepan of simmering water until smooth (don't let water touch base of bowl). Pour mixture into pastry case. Refrigerate tart 2 hours or until firm.

7 Soften the smooth side of the chocolate block slightly by holding your hand on the surface for about a minute; carefully drag a cheese slicer, or large sharp knife, across the back of the chocolate block to make chocolate curls.

8 Serve tart topped with fresh raspberries and chocolate curls.

HAZELNUT PASTRY Process nuts until fine. Add flour, sugar and butter; process until crumbly. With motor operating, add egg yolk and enough of the water so that ingredients just come together. Wrap pastry in plastic wrap; refrigerate 30 minutes.

tip We used frangelico, a hazelnut-flavoured liqueur, for this recipe, but you can use your favourite brand.

passionfruit tart with orange mascarpone cream

PREP + COOK TIME 1½ HOURS (+ REFRIGERATION & COOLING) | SERVES 8

You need about 10 passionfruit for this recipe.

½ cup (80g) pure icing (confectioners') sugar

1 cup (150g) plain (all-purpose) flour

75g (2½ ounces) cold unsalted butter, chopped coarsely

1 egg yolk

1 teaspoon vanilla extract

1 tablespoon iced water

⅔ cup (160ml) passionfruit pulp

300ml (½ pint) pouring cream

½ cup (110g) caster (superfine) sugar

4 eggs

ORANGE MASCARPONE CREAM

250g (8 ounces) mascarpone cheese

¼ cup (60ml) double (thick) cream

2 tablespoons icing (confectioners') sugar

2 tablespoons finely grated orange rind

1 To make pastry, blend or process sugar, flour and butter until crumbly. Add egg yolk, extract and the water; process until ingredients just come together. Wrap pastry in plastic wrap; refrigerate 30 minutes.

2 Grease a 26cm (10½-inch) round loose-based fluted flan pan. Roll pastry between sheets of baking paper until large enough to line pan. Lift pastry into pan, press into base and side; trim excess pastry. Prick base all over with fork. Cover; refrigerate 20 minutes.

3 Preheat oven to 200°C/400°F.

4 Place pan on an oven tray. Line pastry with baking paper; fill with dried beans or rice. Bake 10 minutes. Remove paper and beans. Bake a further 10 minutes or until pastry is golden; cool.

5 Meanwhile, reserve ¼ cup passionfruit pulp. Strain remaining pulp, reserving 2 tablespoons seeds. Whisk cream, sugar and eggs together in a medium bowl; stir in strained passionfruit juice and reserved seeds.

6 Reduce oven temperature to 170°C/325°F. Pour egg mixture into pastry case. Bake about 35 minutes or until set. Cool; refrigerate 3 hours or overnight.

7 Make orange mascarpone cream. Serve tart topped with mascarpone cream; drizzle with reserved passionfruit pulp.

ORANGE MASCARPONE CREAM Combine ingredients in a small bowl.

plum cake

PREP + COOK TIME 2 HOURS (+ COOLING) | SERVES 8

120g (4 ounces) unsalted butter, softened

1½ cups (330g) caster (superfine) sugar

2 eggs

2½ cups (375g) self-raising flour

½ cup (75g) plain (all-purpose) flour

¼ cup (20g) flaked almonds

PLUM FILLING

1.5kg (3 pounds) red-fleshed plums

½ cup (110g) firmly packed light brown sugar

1 Make plum filling.

2 Meanwhile, beat butter and sugar in a small bowl with an electric mixer until light and fluffy. Beat in eggs, one at a time. Transfer mixture to a large bowl; add sifted flours, stir until dough comes together.

3 Grease a closed 25cm (10-inch) round springform pan; line base with baking paper. Press two-thirds of the dough over the base and two-thirds of the way up the side of the pan; fill with plums. Roll out remaining one-third of the dough; place over plums, turning excess dough back to sit over top of cake. Sprinkle over nuts.

4 Bake, uncovered, 20 minutes. Cover cake with foil; bake a further 40 minutes or until cake is golden and a skewer inserted along the sides of the cake comes out clean. Cool in pan on wire rack. Serve dusted with sifted icing sugar, if you like.

PLUM FILLING Preheat oven to 200°C/400°F. Halve plums; discard seeds. Place plums, cut-side up, in a single layer, in a large roasting dish; sprinkle with sugar. Roast about 25 minutes or until plums are tender. Remove plums with a slotted spoon; place on a large plate. Pour pan juices into a small bowl.

tips It's important to measure the springform pan when it's closed; the measurement that appears on the base of springform pans sometimes refers to the measurement of the pan when it is open. We covered the cake loosely with a sheet of foil after 20 minutes to prevent the nuts from burning. Try this cake with other fillings such as apple or pear. The cake is best made on the day of serving.

serving suggestion Double (thick) cream, custard or vanilla ice-cream.

rhubarb and strawberry tarts

PREP + COOK TIME 1¼ HOURS (+ REFRIGERATION & COOLING) | MAKES 8

500g (1 pound) rhubarb

1 cup (220g) caster (superfine) sugar

2 cups (500ml) water

1 teaspoon powdered gelatine

300g (9½ ounces) small strawberries

PASTRY

1¾ cups (260g) plain (all-purpose) flour

125g (4 ounces) cold butter, chopped coarsely

½ cup (110g) caster sugar (superfine)

1 egg, beaten lightly

CUSTARD

2 eggs

1 cup (250ml) milk

1 tablespoon raw sugar

1 Make pastry.

2 Grease eight 10cm (4-inch) round loose-based fluted flan pans. Divide pastry into 8 portions. Roll each portion between sheets of baking paper until large enough to line pans. Lift pastry into pans, press into base and sides; trim excess pastry. Prick bases all over with a fork. Cover; refrigerate 30 minutes.

3 Preheat oven to 180°C/350°F.

4 Place pans on an oven tray. Bake pastry cases about 15 minutes or until golden. Cool.

5 Meanwhile, trim rhubarb; cut into 1cm (½-inch) slices. Combine rhubarb, sugar and the water in a medium saucepan; stir, over medium heat, without boiling, until sugar dissolves. Simmer, uncovered, about 15 minutes or until rhubarb is tender. Drain rhubarb; reserve 1 cup strained syrup. Sprinkle gelatine over hot reserved syrup; stir until dissolved.

6 Make custard.

7 Divide rhubarb into pastry case; pour over custard. Bake tarts about 15 minutes or until set. Cool.

8 Slice strawberries thinly. Top tarts with strawberries; pour 1 tablespoon rhubarb syrup over each tart. Refrigerate 1 hour.

PASTRY Sift flour into a large bowl; rub in butter with fingertips until mixture is crumbly. Stir in sugar, then egg until pastry just comes together. Knead dough on a lightly floured surface until smooth. Flatten dough slightly, wrap in plastic wrap; refrigerate 30 minutes.

CUSTARD Whisk eggs, milk and sugar in a medium bowl until combined.

tip Pastry cases can be made a day ahead; keep in an airtight container at room temperature. Fill on the day of serving.

CAFÉ CAKES

rich red wine chocolate cake

PREP + COOK TIME 1 HOUR (+ COOLING) | SERVES 12

125g (4 ounces) butter, softened

1 cup (220g) caster (superfine) sugar

2 eggs

¾ cup (110g) self-raising flour

¾ cup (110g) plain (all-purpose) flour

⅓ cup (35g) cocoa powder

⅓ cup (80ml) water

⅔ cup (160ml) dry red wine

90g (3 ounces) dark (semi-sweet) chocolate, grated finely

RED WINE MUSCATEL SYRUP

2 cups (440g) caster (superfine) sugar

1½ cups (375ml) dry red wine

1½ cups (375ml) water

250g (8 ounces) dried muscatel clusters

1 Preheat oven to 160°C/325°F. Grease 22cm (9-inch) baba cake pan well.

2 Beat butter and sugar in a small bowl with an electric mixer until light and fluffy. Beat in eggs, one at a time, until combined. Transfer mixture to a large bowl; stir in sifted flours and cocoa, and the water, wine and chocolate.

3 Spread mixture into pan; bake about 50 minutes. Stand cake in pan 5 minutes before turning onto a wire rack to cool.

4 Meanwhile, make red wine muscatel syrup.

5 Top cake with muscatels, drizzle with syrup. Accompany cake with any remaining syrup, and whipped cream, if you like.

RED WINE MUSCATEL SYRUP Stir sugar, wine and the water in a small saucepan over medium heat, without boiling, until sugar dissolves. Cut muscatels into 12 small bunches, add to syrup; bring to the boil. Boil, uncovered, about 15 minutes or until syrup is reduced by one-third and is thickened slightly. Cool.

These striking caramel hazelnuts
are really eye-catching, adding an extra dimension to
this famous European layered cake. Originating
in Hungry in 1885, the torte is named after the pastry chef
who created it, Jozsef Dobos. The success of this
cake was Dobos' invention of butter cream –
for which we are all thankful – and the use of a toffee
covering on top, which kept the cake
fresher for longer.

dobos torte (recipe page 32)

dobos torte

PREP + COOK TIME 2 HOURS (+ COOLING & REFRIGERATION) | SERVES 16

375g (12 ounces) unsalted butter, softened

2 cups (440g) caster (superfine) sugar

3 eggs, separated

3 egg whites

2 cups (300g) self-raising flour

1 cup (150g) plain (all-purpose) flour

1 cup (250ml) milk

CHOCOLATE BUTTER CREAM

250g (8 ounces) dark (semi-sweet) chocolate

4 egg whites

1 cup (220g) caster (superfine) sugar

375g (12 ounces) unsalted butter, softened

CARAMEL HAZELNUTS

24 hazelnuts

1 cup (220g) caster (superfine) sugar

⅓ cup (80ml) water

(pictured on pages 30-31)

1 Preheat oven to 180°C/350°F. Grease three deep 20cm (8-inch) round cake pans. Line bases and sides with baking paper.

2 Beat butter and sugar in a large bowl with an electric mixer until light and fluffy. Beat in egg yolks, one at a time. Beat in sifted flours and milk, in two batches.

3 Beat all the egg whites in a large bowl with an electric mixer until soft peaks form. Fold egg whites into cake mixture.

4 Spread mixture evenly into pans. Bake about 30 minutes. Stand cakes in pans 5 minutes before turning, top-side up, onto wire racks to cool.

5 Make chocolate butter cream and caramel hazelnuts.

6 Using a serrated knife, trim tops of cakes so they are level. Split each cake into three layers (see '*how to split a cake into even layers*', page 113). Place one cake layer on a serving plate; spread with ⅓ cup of butter cream. Repeat with remaining cake layers and butter cream, finishing with a cake layer (to make nine layers). Spread the remaining butter cream over top and side of cake. Refrigerate 30 minutes.

7 Serve torte topped with caramel hazelnuts.

CHOCOLATE BUTTER CREAM Melt chocolate; cool to room temperature. Combine egg whites and sugar in a medium heatproof bowl; whisk over a medium saucepan of simmering water (don't let water touch base of bowl) until sugar dissolves and mixture is warm to touch. Remove from heat. Transfer mixture to a large bowl. Beat egg white mixture with an electric mixer until firm peaks form and mixture cools to room temperature. Gradually beat in butter and then chocolate until smooth.

CARAMEL HAZELNUTS Preheat oven to 180°C/350°F. Place nuts on an oven tray; roast 8 minutes or until skins split. Place in a clean tea towel; rub off skins. Bend the top third of 12 toothpicks over so they snap, but don't break off (see 'how to make caramel hazelnuts', page 113); push the nuts onto the tips. Tie kitchen string between two heavy jars; place baking paper underneath. Stir sugar and the water in a small saucepan over medium heat, without boiling, until sugar dissolves. Bring to the boil; boil, uncovered, without stirring, about 10 minutes or until a medium golden colour. Remove from the heat; allow bubbles to subside. Dip nuts, one at a time, into caramel, then hook end of toothpick over the string, allowing caramel to drip off the nuts into long spikes. Stand at room temperature until set; remove toothpicks.

tips You will need 12 toothpicks. The butter and chocolate for the butter cream must be at room temperature otherwise they will not combine with the egg white when beaten. Unless otherwise indicated, butter and eggs should be at room temperature for baking.

When baking three cakes, place two cake pans on the top oven shelf and one pan on the shelf beneath. Change the position of the pans halfway through the baking time, placing the top pans on the shelf beneath (also placing the pan that was at the back of the oven nearer the oven door) and the remaining pan on the top shelf. This is necessary to allowing for even baking.

baklava torte

PREP + COOK TIME 1¼ HOURS (+ COOLING) | SERVES 12

250g (8 ounces) butter, softened

½ teaspoon almond essence

1 cup (220g) caster (superfine) sugar

4 eggs

⅓ cup (80ml) milk

1½ cups (225g) self-raising flour

½ cup (60g) ground almonds

1 cup (70g) slivered almonds

1 cup (140g) coarsely chopped unsalted shelled pistachios

1 cup (110g) coarsely chopped walnuts

HONEY LEMON SYRUP

1 cup (220g) caster (superfine) sugar

1 cup (250ml) water

1 tablespoon honey

5cm (2-inch) strip lemon rind

2 tablespoons lemon juice

CINNAMON MASCARPONE CREAM

250g (8 ounces) mascarpone cheese

½ teaspoon ground cinnamon

½ cup (125ml) thickened (heavy) cream

1 Preheat oven to 180°C/350°F. Grease two deep 22cm (9-inch) round cake pans; line bases with baking paper.

2 Beat butter, essence and sugar in a small bowl with an electric mixer until light and fluffy. Beat in eggs, one at a time, until combined. Transfer mixture to a large bowl; stir in milk, sifted flour and ground almonds, in two batches.

3 Spread mixture evenly into pans; sprinkle with combined nuts, press down lightly. Bake about 35 minutes.

4 Meanwhile, make honey lemon syrup.

5 Using a skewer, pierce hot cakes a few times, then drizzle ¼-cup hot syrup over each hot cake. Cool cakes in pan. Cool remaining syrup.

6 Meanwhile, make cinnamon mascarpone cream.

7 Place one cake on a serving platter; top with mascarpone cream, then remaining cake. Serve with remaining cooled syrup.

HONEY LEMON SYRUP Stir sugar, the water, honey and rind in a small saucepan over medium heat, without boiling, until sugar dissolves. Bring to the boil; boil, uncovered, about 5 minutes or until thickened slightly. Remove from heat; stir in juice. Discard rind.

CINNAMON MASCARPONE CREAM Stir ingredients in a small bowl until combined.

chocolate and vanilla napoleon

PREP + COOK TIME 1¾ HOURS (+ FREEZING, COOLING & REFRIGERATION) | SERVES 8

You need a piping bag and a 2cm (¾-inch) plain tube; however, you can also spoon the crème pâtissière onto the pastry sheets – just give it a quick stir first.

1 sheet puff pastry

15g (½ ounce) butter

⅔ cup (110g) icing (confectioners') sugar

1 teaspoon glucose syrup

1 tablespoon milk, approximately

2 teaspoons cocoa powder

1 teaspoon water

CRÈME PÂTISSIÈRE

2 cups (500ml) milk

1 teaspoon vanilla bean paste

4 egg yolks

⅓ cup (110g) caster (superfine) sugar

¼ cup (35g) cornflour (cornstarch)

15g (½ ounce) butter

100g (3 ounces) dark (semi-sweet) chocolate, chopped finely

1 Make crème pâtissière.

2 Roll out pastry into a 28cm (11¼-inch) square. Cut pastry into three even rectangles; transfer to a baking-paper-lined oven tray. Prick pastry all over with a fork. Freeze 20 minutes.

3 Preheat oven to 220°C/425°F.

4 Top pastry rectangles with another oven tray (to stop pastry from puffing up). Bake about 15 minutes or until pastry is browned lightly and crisp. Remove top oven tray; cool.

5 To make icing, melt butter; whisk butter, sifted icing sugar, glucose and milk in a small bowl (add a little more milk, if needed, to thin to a drizzling consistency). Transfer 1 tablespoon icing to a small bowl; whisk in sifted cocoa and the water. Spoon chocolate icing into ziptop plastic bag. Snip a tiny piece off one corner.

6 Spread plain icing evenly over one pastry rectangle. Pipe chocolate icing crosswise over plain icing, about 1cm (½-inch) apart. Run the tip of wooden skewer down the length of the iced rectangle in alternate directions to create a decorative pattern.

7 Spoon chocolate crème pâtissière into piping bag fitted with a 2cm (¾ inch) plain tube. Place one uniced pastry rectangle on a serving platter. Pipe chocolate crème pâtissière over the pastry. Top with remaining uniced pastry rectangle, pressing gently to secure. Spoon vanilla crème pâtissière into another piping bag (or clean and dry the bag and tube just used). Pipe crème pâtissière over pastry. Top with iced pastry rectangle, pressing down gently to secure. Refrigerate 1 hour to firm slightly. Cut napoleon into strips using a serrated knife to serve.

CRÈME PÂTISSIÈRE Heat milk and vanilla in a small saucepan over medium heat until almost boiling. Meanwhile, whisk yolks, sugar and cornflour in a medium bowl; gradually whisk in hot milk mixture. Return mixture to pan; whisk over low heat 5 minutes or until thickened. Remove from heat; stir in butter. Divide into two small bowls. Stir chocolate into one until smooth; leave remaining bowl plain. Cover surfaces with plastic wrap; refrigerate until firm.

walnut cake with espresso mascarpone cream

PREP + COOK TIME 1½ HOURS (+ COOLING) | SERVES 8

125g (4 ounces) butter, softened

⅔ cup (150g) raw sugar

3 eggs, separated

1⅓ cups (200g) self-raising flour

1⅓ cups (160g) ground walnuts

⅔ cup (160ml) milk

¼ cup (90g) honey

½ cup (50g) walnut halves, roasted

ESPRESSO MASCARPONE CREAM

250g (8 ounces) mascarpone cheese

1 tablespoon icing (confectioners') sugar

1 tablespoon instant coffee granules

1 tablespoon hot water

1 Preheat oven to 160°C/325°F. Grease deep 20cm (8-inch) round cake pan; line base and side with baking paper.

2 Beat butter and sugar in a small bowl with an electric mixer until light and fluffy. Beat in egg yolks, one at a time, until combined. Transfer mixture to a large bowl; stir in sifted flour, ground walnuts and milk, in two batches.

3 Beat egg whites in a small bowl with an electric mixer until soft peaks form. Fold egg whites into cake mixture.

4 Spread mixture into pan. Bake about 50 minutes. Stand cake in pan 5 minutes before turning, top-side up, onto a wire rack to cool.

5 Meanwhile, make espresso mascarpone cream.

6 Using a serrated knife, split cake into two layers (see 'how to split a cake into even layers', page 113). Place bottom layer on a serving plate; spread with half the espresso cream; top with remaining layer. Warm the honey slightly. Spread top of cake with remaining espresso cream, scatter with walnut halves and drizzle with honey.

ESPRESSO MASCARPONE CREAM Beat mascarpone and sifted icing sugar in a small bowl with a wooden spoon until combined. Dissolve coffee in the hot water in a small cup; fold into mascarpone mixture. Cover; refrigerate until ready to use.

tip To make the ground walnuts, process 1½ cups (150g) roasted walnuts until fine.

PETIT FOURS

mini red velvet whoopie pies

PREP + COOK TIME 1 HOUR (+ COOLING) | MAKES 24

60g (2 ounces) butter, softened

1 egg

½ teaspoon vanilla extract

½ cup (110g) caster (superfine) sugar

¾ cup (110g) plain (all-purpose) flour

1 tablespoon cocoa powder

½ cup (125ml) buttermilk

2 teaspoons red food colouring

½ teaspoon white vinegar

½ teaspoon bicarbonate of soda (baking soda)

2 tablespoons icing (confectioners') sugar

CREAM CHEESE FROSTING

90g (3 ounces) cream cheese, softened

¾ cup (120g) icing (confectioners') sugar

1 teaspoon finely grated lemon rind

1 Preheat oven to 180°C/350°F. Grease two 12-hole (1-tablespoon/20ml) shallow round-based patty pans.

2 Beat butter, egg, extract and caster sugar in a small bowl with an electric mixer until combined. Stir in sifted flour and cocoa, and combined buttermilk and food colouring. Combine vinegar and soda in a small bowl (it will froth slightly). Fold into cake mixture.

3 Drop rounded teaspoons of mixture into each pan hole. Bake about 10 minutes. Immediately tap trays on bench to remove cakes. Transfer to a wire rack to cool.

4 Make cream cheese frosting.

5 Sandwich whoopie pies with cream cheese frosting. Dust pies with sifted icing sugar to serve.

CREAM CHEESE FROSTING Beat ingredients in a small bowl with an electric mixer until smooth.

chocolate, hazelnut and berry petit fours

PREP + COOK TIME 1¼ HOURS (+ COOLING & REFRIGERATION) | MAKES 25

25g (¾ ounce) unsalted butter

4 eggs

4 egg whites

1¼ cups (125g) ground hazelnuts

1 cup (160g) icing (confectioners') sugar

⅓ cup (50g) plain (all-purpose) flour

1 tablespoon caster (superfine) sugar

RASPBERRY JAM

500g (1 pound) frozen raspberries

1 cup (220g) caster (superfine) sugar

1 tablespoon water

HAZELNUT GANACHE

180g (5½ ounces) dark (semi-sweet) chocolate

¼ cup (60ml) pouring cream

1 tablespoon hazelnut-flavoured liqueur

CHOCOLATE GLAZE

180g (5½ ounces) dark (semi-sweet) chocolate

75g (2½ ounces) butter

1 Preheat oven to 220°C/425°F. Grease two 25cm x 30cm x 2.5cm (10-inch x 12-inch x 1-inch) swiss roll pans; line bases with baking paper, extending paper 5cm (2 inches) over long sides.

2 Melt butter. Beat whole eggs, ground hazelnuts and sifted icing sugar in a small bowl with an electric mixer until creamy; beat in sifted flour. Transfer mixture to a large bowl; stir in butter.

3 Beat egg whites in a small bowl with an electric mixer until soft peaks form; add caster sugar, beating until sugar dissolves. Fold egg white mixture into hazelnut mixture, in two batches.

4 Spread mixture evenly into pans. Bake about 7 minutes. Cool sponges in pans.

5 Meanwhile, make raspberry jam and hazelnut ganache.

6 Turn sponges onto board. Using a serrated knife, cut 10cm (4 inches) off the end of each sponge. Place one large sponge on a baking-paper-lined tray; spread with half the raspberry jam; top with half the ganache. Top with the two smaller pieces of sponge; spread with remaining jam and ganache. Top with remaining large sponge. Refrigerate 30 minutes or until ganache is set.

7 Make chocolate glaze.

8 Spread sponge with glaze. Refrigerate about 10 minutes or until set. Using a serrated knife, neatly trim all sides. Cut into 3cm x 4.5cm (1¼-inch x 1¾-inch) bars before serving.

RASPBERRY JAM Combine raspberries, sugar and the water in a small saucepan; stir over medium heat, without boiling, until sugar dissolves. Bring to the boil. Boil, uncovered, stirring occasionally, about 10 minutes or until thick. Cool.

HAZELNUT GANACHE Break chocolate into a medium heatproof bowl, add cream and liqueur; stir over a medium saucepan of simmering water until smooth (don't let water touch base of bowl).

CHOCOLATE GLAZE Break chocolate into a medium heatproof bowl, add butter; stir over a medium saucepan of simmering water until smooth (don't let water touch base of bowl).

mini chocolate ricotta cannoli

PREP + COOK TIME 1 HOUR (+ REFRIGERATION & COOLING) | MAKES 24

You need a pasta machine, cannoli moulds (8cm long and 2cm wide/3¼-inch x ¾-inch) and a piping bag fitted with a 1cm (½-inch) plain tube for this recipe.

50g (1½ ounces) butter

1½ cups (225g) plain (all-purpose) flour

1 egg

2 egg yolks

1 egg white

2 tablespoons marsala, approximately

vegetable oil, for deep-frying

1 tablespoon icing (confectioners') sugar

RICOTTA FILLING

50g (1½ ounces) dark (semi-sweet) chocolate

300g (9½ ounces) ricotta cheese

⅓ cup (55g) icing (confectioners') sugar

250g (8 ounces) mascarpone cheese

1 tablespoon marsala

1 Melt butter; cool. Process flour, butter, egg, egg yolks and enough of the marsala so that ingredients just come together. Knead dough on a floured surface until smooth. Wrap dough in plastic wrap; refrigerate 1 hour.

2 Divide dough in half. Roll each portion through a pasta machine, starting on the widest setting, decreasing settings and dusting lightly with flour between rolling, until 1mm (¹⁄₃₂-inch) thick.

3 Cut 24 x 7.5cm (3-inch) rounds from dough. Wrap rounds around cannoli moulds, brushing overlapping ends with lightly beaten egg white and pressing firmly to seal. (Don't let egg white touch the moulds or cannoli will be hard to remove).

4 Heat oil in a large saucepan to 180°C/350°F (or until a cube of bread turns golden in about 30 seconds); deep-fry cannoli, in batches, until browned and crisp. Drain on absorbent paper. Remove cannoli from moulds while still warm. Repeat with remaining moulds and dough. Cool.

5 Meanwhile, make ricotta filling.

6 Spoon ricotta filling into piping bag fitted with 1cm (½-inch) plain tube. Pipe filling into cannoli shells. Serve dusted with sifted icing sugar.

RICOTTA FILLING Finely grate chocolate. Beat ricotta and sifted icing sugar in a small bowl with an electric mixer until smooth. Fold in mascarpone, marsala and chocolate.

tip Marsala is a sweet, fortified wine (a wine to which additional alcohol has been added, most commonly in the form of brandy). Other common fortified wines include sherry, port and vermouth.

chocolate and coconut dessert friands

PREP + COOK TIME 45 MINUTES | MAKES 9

5 paradise pears (200g)

½ cup (110g) caster (superfine) sugar

2 cups (500ml) water

100g (3 ounces) dark (semi-sweet) chocolate

90g (3 ounces) butter, chopped coarsely

6 egg whites

1 teaspoon vanilla extract

1 cup (80g) desiccated coconut

1 cup (160g) icing (confectioners') sugar

½ cup (75g) plain (all-purpose) flour

CHOCOLATE SAUCE

100g (3 ounces) dark (semi-sweet) chocolate

¼ cup (60ml) pouring cream

25g (1 ounce) butter

1 tablespoon walnut or hazelnut-flavoured liqueur

1 Peel and halve pears. Place sugar and the water in a small saucepan, add pears; bring to the boil. Reduce heat; simmer, covered, about 20 minutes or until pears are tender.

2 Preheat oven to 200°C/400°F. Grease 9-hole (½-cup/125ml) oval friand pan. Place pan on an oven tray.

3 Break chocolate into a medium heatproof bowl; add butter. Place over a medium saucepan of simmering water (don't let water touch base of bowl); stir until smooth. Cool 5 minutes. Whisk egg whites in a medium bowl until frothy; add chocolate mixture, extract, coconut, and sifted icing sugar and flour, stir until combined.

4 Divide mixture evenly into pan holes; top each with a pear half, cut-side up. Bake about 20 minutes. Stand friands in pan 5 minutes before turning, top-side up, onto a wire rack to cool.

5 Make chocolate sauce.

6 Serve friands with warm chocolate sauce.

CHOCOLATE SAUCE Break chocolate into a medium heatproof bowl, add cream and butter; stir over medium saucepan of simmering water until smooth (don't let water touch base of bowl). Stir in liqueur.

tips We used chocolate with a 70% cocoa content. If paradise pears are unavailable, substitute 5 canned pear halves and omit step 1.

mini polenta and raspberry cakes

PREP + COOK TIME 50 MINUTES (+ COOLING) | MAKES 18

45g (1½ ounces) butter, softened

1 egg

1 teaspoon finely grated orange rind

⅓ cup (55g) polenta (cornmeal)

¼ cup (55g) raw caster (superfine) sugar

2 tablespoons milk

½ cup (60g) ground almonds

½ teaspoon baking powder

⅓ cup (50g) frozen raspberries

18 fresh raspberries

GLACÉ ICING

¼ cup (40g) frozen raspberries, thawed

¾ cup (120g) icing (confectioners') sugar

1 teaspoon butter, softened

1 Preheat oven to 180°C/350°F. Grease 18 holes of two 12-hole (1-tablespoon/20ml) mini muffin or bordeaux cake pans.

2 Beat butter, egg, rind, polenta and sugar in a small bowl with an electric mixer until light and fluffy. Stir in milk, ground almonds, baking powder and frozen raspberries.

3 Divide mixture evenly between pan holes. Bake about 20 minutes. Stand cakes in pans 5 minutes before turning onto a wire rack to cool.

4 Meanwhile, make glacé icing. Spread cold cakes with icing; top with fresh raspberries.

GLACÉ ICING Push raspberries through a fine sieve into a small bowl; discard seeds. Add sifted icing sugar and butter; stir to combine.

tip Bordeaux cake pans are typically used to make a small specialty cake of the Bordeaux region in France called a 'canelle'. Those made from silicon are the easiest to work with.

cherry tarts

PREP + COOK TIME 1½ HOURS (+ REFRIGERATION) | MAKES 12

1¼ cups (185g) plain (all-purpose) flour

2 tablespoons caster (superfine) sugar

¼ cup (30g) ground almonds

125g (4 ounces) cold butter, chopped coarsely

1 egg yolk

2 tablespoons iced water

¼ cup (80g) cherry jam

½ cup (80g) icing (confectioners') sugar

ALMOND FILLING

90g (3 ounces) butter, softened

⅔ cup (150g) caster (superfine) sugar

1 tablespoon finely grated lemon rind

2 eggs

¼ cup (35g) plain (all-purpose) flour

1 cup (120g) ground almonds

1 Blend or process flour, sugar, ground almonds and butter until crumbly. Add egg yolk and the water; process until ingredients just come together. Wrap pastry in plastic wrap; refrigerate 30 minutes.

2 Preheat oven to 200°C/400°F.

3 Grease 12 x 4cm (1½-inch) individual fluted brioche tins. Roll pastry between sheets of baking paper until 3mm (⅛-inch) thick. Cut 12 x 9.5cm (4-inch) rounds from pastry. Press pastry rounds into tins.

4 Make almond filling.

5 Spoon a little jam into the base of each pastry case. Top with almond filling; smooth tops. Bake about 20 minutes or until tarts are firm to touch and browned lightly. Stand tarts in tins 5 minutes before turning, top-side up, onto a wire rack to cool.

6 Dust tarts generously with sifted icing sugar before serving.

ALMOND FILLING Beat butter, sugar and rind in a small bowl with an electric mixer until light and fluffy. Beat in eggs, one at a time. Beat in sifted flour and ground almonds until combined.

tip To make a cross pattern on the tarts, dust tarts generously with sifted icing sugar, then carefully heat a metal skewer over a flame (from a gas-stove top or a cook's blowtorch). Sear a cross pattern into the top of each tart with the heated skewer before serving.

mini french éclairs with praline

PREP + COOK TIME 1½ HOURS (+ COOLING & STANDING) | MAKES 24

You need a piping bag fitted with a 1cm (½-inch) plain tube for this recipe.

½ cup (125ml) water

60g (2 ounces) cold butter, chopped finely

1 tablespoon caster (superfine) sugar

½ cup (75g) baker's flour

3 eggs

100g (3 ounces) dark (semi-sweet) chocolate

PRALINE

⅓ cup (45g) hazelnuts

¾ cup (165g) caster (superfine) sugar

1 tablespoon water

CRÈME PÂTISSIÈRE

⅓ cup (80ml) milk

⅓ cup (80ml) pouring cream

1 vanilla bean

1 egg yolk

1 tablespoon caster (superfine) sugar

1 tablespoon cornflour (cornstarch)

15g (½ ounce) butter

1 Make praline and crème pâtissière.
2 Preheat oven to 160°C/320°F. Grease oven trays.
3 To make choux pastry, combine the water, butter and sugar in a medium saucepan; bring to the boil. Add flour, beat with wooden spoon over medium heat until mixture comes away from base of pan (see 'making choux pastry', page 113). Transfer pastry to a medium bowl; beat in two of the eggs, one at a time. Whisk remaining egg with a fork, beat enough of the egg into the pastry until it becomes smooth and glossy but still holds its shape.

4 Spoon mixture into a piping bag fitted with a 1cm (½-inch) plain tube. Pipe 5cm (2-inch) lengths of choux pastry, about 3cm (1¼ inches) apart, onto trays; bake about 15 minutes. Cut a small opening into the base of each éclair; bake a further 5 minutes or until éclairs are dry. Cool on trays.
5 Break chocolate into a medium heatproof bowl, stir over a medium saucepan of simmering water until melted. Dip the top of each éclair into the chocolate; stand on wire racks until set.
6 Cut éclairs in half lengthways. Lightly stir crème pâtissière then spoon 3 teaspoons of custard into each éclair; top with praline to serve.

PRALINE Spread nuts over a baking-paper-lined oven tray. Stir sugar and the water in a small saucepan over medium heat, without boiling, until sugar dissolves. Bring to the boil. Reduce heat; simmer, uncovered, without stirring, until a golden caramel colour. Pour caramel over nuts. Stand until set. Blend or process praline until it resembles fine breadcrumbs.

CRÈME PÂTISSIÈRE Combine milk and cream in a medium saucepan. Split vanilla bean in half lengthways; scrape seeds into pan, then add bean. Bring mixture almost to the boil; discard bean. Meanwhile, whisk egg yolk, sugar and cornflour in a medium bowl until combined. Gradually whisk hot milk mixture into egg mixture; return custard to pan. Cook over low heat, stirring, until mixture boils and thickens; remove from heat. Transfer custard to a medium bowl; stir in butter. Cover surface with plastic wrap; refrigerate until firm.

white chocolate and cherry cheesecakes

PREP + COOK TIME 1½ HOURS (+ REFRIGERATION) | MAKES 12

60g (2 ounces) unsalted butter

150g (4½ ounces) Scottish shortbread biscuits

12 cherries (110g)

WHITE CHOCOLATE FILLING

125g (4 ounces) white chocolate

250g (8 ounces) cream cheese, softened

½ cup (125ml) pouring cream

2 eggs

2 tablespoons caster (superfine) sugar

1 Grease 12 x 4cm (1½-inch) loose-based (¼-cup/60ml) mini cheesecake pans.

2 Melt butter; cool. Process biscuits until fine; add butter, process until combined. Divide mixture into pans, pressing firmly over bases. Refrigerate 30 minutes.

3 Preheat oven to 150°C/300°F.

4 Bake cheesecake bases about 10 minutes. Cool in pans.

5 Make white chocolate filling.

6 Divide filling into each pan. Bake cheesecakes about 15 minutes (when they are cooked, they should wobble like jelly when the tray is gently shaken). Cool in oven with the door ajar.

7 Lightly push a cherry into the top of each cheesecake. Refrigerate 2 hours.

WHITE CHOCOLATE FILLING Break chocolate into a medium heatproof bowl. Place bowl over a medium saucepan of simmering water (don't let water touch base of bowl); stir until smooth. Beat cream cheese in a small bowl with an electric mixer until smooth. Add cream, eggs and sugar, beat just until combined. Stir in melted chocolate.

tip If you use shortbread biscuits other than the Scottish variety used here, you may need to increase the amount of melted butter by about 20g (¾ ounce) so that the biscuit base will set.

rum babas

PREP + COOK TIME 1 HOUR (+ STANDING, COOLING & REFRIGERATION) | MAKES 48

½ cup (125ml) milk

2 teaspoons dried yeast (7g)

1 tablespoon raw sugar

1¾ cups (260g) plain (all-purpose) flour

2 eggs

80g (2½ ounces) butter, softened

2 tablespoons sultanas

RUM SYRUP

1 litre (4 cups) water

2 cups (440g) caster (superfine) sugar

1 vanilla bean

2 cinnamon sticks

2 slices lime

2 slices orange

½ cup (125ml) dark rum

1 Warm milk in a small saucepan. Whisk yeast, warmed milk and sugar in a large bowl until combined. Cover; stand in a warm place about 10 minutes or until frothy.

2 Add sifted flour and eggs to yeast mixture; mix to a soft dough. Knead dough on a floured surface about 10 minutes or until smooth and elastic. Place in a lightly oiled large bowl, cover; stand in a warm place about 1 hour or until doubled in size.

3 Grease four 12-hole (1-tablespoon/20ml) mini muffin pans.

4 Mix butter and sultanas into dough; knead on a floured surface until combined. Roll 1 rounded teaspoon of dough into a ball and place in each a pan hole. Cover pans; stand in a warm place for about 1 hour or until doubled in size.

5 Preheat oven to 160°C/320°F.

6 Bake babas about 20 minutes or until browned lightly; cool in pans.

7 Meanwhile, make rum syrup.

8 Place babas in a large heatproof bowl; pour over hot syrup. Stand at room temperature 1 hour for syrup to soak in; refrigerate 1 hour before serving.

RUM SYRUP Stir the water, sugar, vanilla bean, cinnamon, lime and orange in a large saucepan over medium heat, without boiling, until sugar dissolves. Bring to the boil. Reduce heat; simmer, uncovered, without stirring, 8 minutes. Remove from heat; stir in rum.

MOUTHFULS

coffee cakes

PREP + COOK TIME 50 MINUTES (+ COOLING) | MAKES 36

125g (4 ounces) butter, softened

½ cup (110g) raw sugar

2 eggs, separated

3 teaspoons instant coffee granules

1 tablespoon hot water

⅔ cup (100g) self-raising flour

2 tablespoons milk

COFFEE ICING

2 teaspoons instant coffee granules

1 tablespoon hot water

1 cup (160g) icing (confectioners') sugar

1 Preheat oven to 160°C/325°F. Grease three 12-hole (1-tablespoon/20ml) mini muffin pans.

2 Beat butter and sugar in a medium bowl with an electric mixer until light and fluffy. Beat in egg yolks, one at a time, until combined. Stir coffee and the hot water in a small cup until coffee dissolves. Stir sifted flour, milk and coffee mixture into butter mixture.

3 Beat egg whites in a small bowl with an electric mixer until soft peaks form. Fold egg whites into cake mixture.

4 Spoon 2 teaspoons of mixture into each pan hole. Bake about 20 minutes. Cool cakes in pans 5 minutes before turning, top-side down, onto a wire rack to cool.

5 Meanwhile, make coffee icing. Spread cold cake bases with icing, allowing it to drip a little down the side.

COFFEE ICING Stir coffee and the hot water in a small cup until coffee dissolves. Sift icing sugar into a small bowl; gradually stir in the coffee until icing is smooth.

cointreau fruit mince, ginger and chocolate tarts

PREP + COOK TIME 1 HOUR (+ STANDING & REFRIGERATION) | MAKES 24

½ cup (80g) mixed dried fruit

¼ cup (60ml) orange-flavoured liqueur

GINGERBREAD

60g (2 ounces) cold butter

1½ cups (225g) plain (all-purpose) flour

½ teaspoon bicarbonate of soda (baking soda)

⅓ cup (75g) firmly packed light brown sugar

2 teaspoons ground ginger

½ teaspoon ground cinnamon

¼ teaspoon ground cloves

2 tablespoons treacle

1 egg

DARK CHOCOLATE GANACHE

150g (4½ ounces) dark (semi-sweet) chocolate, chopped coarsely

¼ cup (60ml) pouring cream

25g (¾ ounce) butter

CARAMEL SHARDS

¼ cup (55g) caster (superfine) sugar

¼ cup (60ml) water

1 Finely chop fruit. Combine fruit and liqueur in a small bowl, cover; stand overnight.

2 Make gingerbread.

3 Divide gingerbread dough in half. Roll each portion of dough, separately, between sheets of baking paper until 3mm (⅛-inch) thick. Place on baking paper-lined trays; refrigerate 30 minutes.

4 Preheat oven to 180°C/350°F. Grease two 12-hole (1-tablespoon/20ml) shallow round-based patty pans.

5 Cut 24 x 6.5cm (2¾-inch) rounds from dough; press into pan holes. Bake about 8 minutes. Cool in pans.

6 Meanwhile, make ganache.

7 Spoon fruit mixture into gingerbread cases; pour over ganache, smooth surface. Refrigerate 1 hour or until set.

8 Meanwhile, make caramel shards. Sprinkle tarts with caramel shards just before serving.

GINGERBREAD Coarsely chop butter. Process flour, soda, sugar, spices and chopped butter until crumbly. Add treacle and egg; process until ingredients come together. Wrap in plastic wrap; refrigerate 30 minutes.

DARK CHOCOLATE GANACHE Stir chocolate, cream and butter in a medium heatproof bowl over a medium saucepan of simmering water until smooth (don't let water touch base of bowl).

CARAMEL SHARDS Stir sugar and the water in a small saucepan over medium heat, without boiling, until sugar dissolves. Bring to the boil. Boil, uncovered, without stirring, about 5 minutes or until a golden colour. Pour caramel onto baking-paper-lined oven tray. Stand until set. Chop caramel into shards.

chocolate and rosewater turkish delight bites

PREP + COOK TIME 1 HOUR (+ STANDING & REFRIGERATION) | MAKES 36

You need a sugar (candy) thermometer for this recipe.

¼ cup (45g) powdered gelatine

¼ cup (60ml) water

3 cups (660g) caster (superfine) sugar

2 cups (500ml) water, extra

¾ cup (110g) cornflour (cornstarch)

2 tablespoons glucose syrup

2 tablespoons rosewater

red food colouring

360g (11½ ounces) dark (semi-sweet) chocolate

¼ cup (20g) flaked almonds

1 Grease deep 17cm (6¾-inch) square cake pan.

2 Sprinkle gelatine over the water in a small heatproof bowl; stand bowl in a small saucepan of simmering water. Stir until gelatine dissolves.

3 Stir sugar and ¾ cup of the extra water in a medium saucepan over medium heat, without boiling, until sugar dissolves. Bring to the boil. Boil, uncovered, without stirring, until temperature of the syrup reaches 116°C/240°F (soft ball stage) on a sugar thermometer. Simmer at 116°C for 5 minutes, without stirring, regulating heat to maintain temperature at 116°C. Remove pan from heat.

4 Meanwhile, place cornflour in another medium saucepan; gradually stir in the remaining extra water. Bring to the boil, stirring, until the mixture thickens.

5 Gradually whisk hot sugar syrup, gelatine mixture and glucose into the cornflour mixture; bring to the boil. Reduce heat; simmer, stirring, about 10 minutes or until mixture thickens a little more. Remove pan from heat; whisk in rosewater, tint with colouring.

6 Strain mixture through a fine sieve into cake pan; skim any scum from surface. Stand 15 minutes; cover surface with lightly greased baking paper, stand 3 hours or overnight to set.

7 Melt chocolate. Turn turkish delight onto a board; cut into squares with an oiled knife. Using a fork, dip squares into chocolate, drain off excess; place on baking-paper-lined tray, sprinkle tops with nuts. Refrigerate 1 hour or until chocolate sets.

berry jam and vanilla palmiers

PREP + COOK TIME 20 MINUTES (+ FREEZING & COOLING) | MAKES 46

½ cup (60g) flaked almonds, chopped very finely

1 teaspoon vanilla bean paste

1 teaspoon finely grated orange rind

⅔ cup (215g) berry jam

2 sheets puff pastry

2 tablespoons caster (superfine) sugar

1 Combine nuts, vanilla, rind and jam in a small bowl.

2 Spread jam mixture evenly over pastry sheets. Fold two opposite sides of pastry inwards to meet in the middle; flatten slightly. Repeat fold again and flatten slightly. Fold again so the outside edges of pastry meet. Roll pastry in sugar, then wrap, separately, in plastic wrap; freeze 30 minutes or until slightly firm.

3 Preheat oven to 180°C/350°F. Line oven trays with baking paper.

4 Discard plastic wrap from pastry; cut pastry into 1cm (½-inch) slices. Place slices, cut-side up, 5cm (2 inches) apart on trays. Bake about 20 minutes or until puffed and golden. Cool on trays.

lemon marshmallows

PREP + COOK TIME 1¼ HOURS (+ REFRIGERATION) | MAKES 24

2 tablespoons (28g) powdered gelatine

¼ cup (60ml) water

1 cup (250ml) boiling water

2 cups (440g) caster (superfine) sugar

¼ cup (60ml) limoncello liqueur

1 teaspoon vanilla extract

1 teaspoon lemon essence

2 teaspoons lemon juice

yellow food colouring

1½ cups (120g) desiccated coconut

1 Sprinkle gelatine over the water; stir to combine.
2 Stir the boiling water and sugar in a medium saucepan over heat, without boiling, until sugar dissolves. Bring to the boil; stir in gelatine mixture and liqueur. Boil, uncovered, about 20 minutes. Remove from heat; cool slightly.
3 Pour mixture into the medium bowl of an electric mixer, add extract, essence and juice; beat on high speed until very thick and white. Tint marshmallow mixture yellow with colouring.
4 Rinse deep 20cm (8-inch) square cake pan with cold water; do not wipe dry. Pour marshmallow mixture into pan; refrigerate about 3 hours or until set.
5 Using a wet knife, and with the marshmallow still in the pan, cut into 24 squares. Carefully lift marshmallows from pan using a small spatula; toss in coconut.

tip Marshmallows are best eaten on the day they are made when they are at their softest. They will keep, refrigerated, in an airtight container for up to a week, but do become more firm during this time.
Limoncello is made from the peel only of fragrant lemons. The peel is soaked in a good-quality clear alcohol then diluted with sugar and water.

little sultana scrolls

PREP + COOK TIME 1½ HOURS (+ REFRIGERATION & FREEZING) | MAKES 36

250g (8 ounces) cold unsalted butter, chopped coarsely

250g (8 ounces) cream cheese, chopped coarsely

¼ cup (55g) caster (superfine) sugar

2¼ cups (335g) plain (all-purpose) flour

2 egg yolks

¼ cup (55g) demerara sugar

SULTANA FILLING

500g (1 pound) sultanas

1½ cups (375ml) water

¼ cup (55g) caster (superfine) sugar

1 teaspoon ground cinnamon

1 teaspoon vanilla extract

1 cup (120g) finely chopped walnuts

¼ cup (60ml) dark rum

1 Make sultana filling.

2 Process butter, cream cheese, caster sugar and flour until ingredients come together. Knead dough on floured surface until smooth. Divide pastry into two portions. Wrap separately in plastic wrap; refrigerate 1 hour.

3 Using one portion of pastry at a time, roll the pastry between sheets of baking paper into a 35cm (14-inch) square. Cut pastry in half; spread both halves evenly using half the sultana filling, leaving a 1cm (½ inch) border all around. Starting from one long side, roll up dough to form a log, flatten slightly. Repeat with remaining dough and filling. Wrap logs, separately, in plastic wrap; freeze 15 minutes.

4 Preheat oven to 190°C/375°F. Line oven trays with baking paper.

5 Cut logs into 3cm (1¼-inch) slices. Place on trays, about 4cm (1½ inches) apart. Brush with lightly beaten egg yolk; sprinkle with demerara sugar. Bake about 25 minutes or until browned lightly. Stand on trays 5 minutes before transferring to a wire rack to cool.

SULTANA FILLING Combine sultanas, the water, sugar, cinnamon and extract in a medium saucepan; bring to the boil. Reduce heat; simmer, uncovered, about 10 minutes or until sultanas are plump and water has almost evaporated. Process sultana mixture until almost smooth. Add nuts; process until mixture forms a paste. Stir in rum; cool.

lemon and basil macaroons

PREP + COOK TIME 1½ HOURS (+ REFRIGERATION, STANDING & COOLING) | MAKES 20

You need three eggs for this recipe — 3 yolks for the curd and 3 whites for the macaroons. You also need a piping bag fitted with a 2cm (¾-inch) plain tube.

3 egg whites

¼ cup (55g) caster (superfine) sugar

1¼ cups (200g) icing (confectioners') sugar

1 cup (120g) ground almonds

LEMON AND BASIL CURD

16 medium basil leaves, torn

3 egg yolks

2 tablespoons caster (superfine) sugar

2 teaspoons finely grated lemon rind

2 tablespoons lemon juice

30g (1 ounce) butter

1 Make lemon and basil curd.

2 Grease oven trays; line with baking paper.

3 Beat egg whites in a small bowl with an electric mixer until soft peaks form. Add caster sugar; beat until sugar dissolves. Transfer mixture to a large bowl. Fold sifted icing sugar and ground almonds into egg-white mixture, in two batches.

4 Spoon mixture into piping bag fitted with a 2cm (¾-inch) plain tube. Pipe 4cm (1½-inch) rounds, about 2cm (¾ inch) apart, onto trays. Tap trays on bench so macaroons spread slightly. Stand 30 minutes.

5 Meanwhile, preheat oven to 150°C/300°F.

6 Bake macaroons about 20 minutes. Cool on trays.

7 Sandwich macaroons with curd.

LEMON AND BASIL CURD Place 12 of the basil leaves, egg yolks, sugar, rind, juice and butter in a small heatproof bowl; stir over a small saucepan of simmering water until mixture thickens slightly and coats the back of a spoon. Remove from heat; strain curd into a small bowl, discard basil. Add the remaining basil leaves, cover; refrigerate curd until cold.

tip For a flavour variation, you can use lime rind and juice instead of lemon or use coriander instead of basil.

salted pistachio truffles

PREP + COOK TIME 45 MINUTES (+ REFRIGERATION) | MAKES 24

200g (6½ ounces) milk chocolate

2 tablespoons thickened (heavy) cream

1 teaspoon vanilla extract

½ cup (70g) finely chopped unsalted pistachios

¼ teaspoon sea salt flakes

1 Break chocolate into a small saucepan, add cream; stir over low heat until smooth. Stir in vanilla. Transfer mixture to a small bowl, cover; refrigerate 3 hours or overnight.

2 Working with a quarter of the chocolate mixture at a time (keep remainder in refrigerator), roll rounded teaspoons of mixture into balls; place on a baking-paper-lined tray. Refrigerate truffles until firm.

3 Working quickly, roll balls in combined nuts and salt, return to tray; refrigerate until firm.

pistachio and raspberry mignardises

PREP + COOK TIME 30 MINUTES | MAKES 24

185g (6 ounces) butter

6 egg whites

1 cup (120g) ground almonds

1½ cups (240g) icing (confectioners') sugar

¾ cup (110g) plain (all-purpose) flour

1 tablespoon unsalted shelled pistachios, chopped finely

100g (3 ounces) fresh or frozen raspberries

1 Preheat oven to 180°C/ 350°F. Grease two 12-hole (1-tablespoon/20ml) mini muffin pans.

2 Melt butter; cool. Whisk egg whites in a medium bowl until frothy. Add butter, ground almonds, sifted icing sugar and flour; stir until combined.

3 Divide mixture into pan holes; sprinkle with nuts, top each with a raspberry.

4 Bake about 15 minutes. Stand mignardise in pans 5 minutes before turning, top-side up, onto wire rack to cool.

tip Mignardises date back to 18th century France, when pastry chefs baked small treats at the end of the day in the low residual heat of their ovens. The name comes from an old French word meaning 'cute', 'graceful', 'pretty'. They are served at the end of the meal to extend the pleasure of the evening.

toffee brittle

PREP + COOK TIME 35 MINUTES (+ STANDING & REFRIGERATION) | MAKES 18

You will need a sugar (candy) thermometer for this recipe.

250g (8 ounces) butter, chopped coarsely

1 cup (220g) caster (superfine) sugar

2 teaspoons water

1 teaspoon vanilla extract

180g (5½ ounces) dark (semi-sweet) chocolate

⅔ cup (90g) roasted unsalted shelled pistachios, chopped finely

1 Stir butter, sugar and the water in a medium heavy-based saucepan over low heat until sugar is dissolved and butter melted. Bring to the boil, stirring occasionally, until toffee mixture reaches 155°C on a sugar thermometer (see *'how to use a sugar thermometer'*, page 113).

2 Remove pan from the heat; allow bubbles to subside. Stir in extract. Drop tablespoonfuls of toffee mixture onto baking-paper-lined trays. Stand until set.

3 Melt chocolate. Dip toffee into chocolate, then in nuts; return to trays. Refrigerate until chocolate is set.

tip If you prefer, you can make one large slab of toffee; pour the toffee mixture onto a baking-paper-lined oven tray and stand until set. Spread the back of the toffee slab with melted chocolate then sprinkle with the nuts. Refrigerate until the chocolate is set, then break toffee into pieces before serving.

rum truffles

PREP + COOK TIME 30 MINUTES (+ REFRIGERATION) | MAKES 24

250g (8 ounces) dark (semi-sweet) chocolate

2 tablespoons milk

75g (2½ ounces) butter

1 tablespoon dark rum

1 cup (100g) cocoa powder

1 Break chocolate into a medium heatproof bowl, add milk and butter; stir over a small saucepan of simmering water until smooth (don't let water touch base of bowl). Stir in rum. Cover with plastic wrap; refrigerate 2 hours.

2 Line tray with baking paper. Sift cocoa powder onto a large tray. Roll rounded teaspoons of mixture into balls; roll in cocoa. Place on baking-paper-lined tray. Refrigerate truffles until firm.

tip If you have one, you can use a melon baller to scoop perfectly round balls of truffle mixture.

BISCUITS & BISCOTTI

chai latte biscotti

PREP + COOK TIME 1½ HOURS (+ COOLING) | MAKES 36

1 english breakfast tea bag

1 cup (150g) plain (all-purpose) flour

¼ cup (35g) self-raising flour

1 teaspoon ground ginger

½ teaspoon each ground cardamom, cinnamon and cloves

½ cup (110g) firmly packed dark brown sugar

1 egg

1 tablespoon honey

½ cup (70g) roasted unsalted shelled pistachios

1 Preheat oven to 180°C/350°F. Grease oven tray.

2 Empty contents of tea bag into processor; process tea with flours and spices until fine.

3 Whisk sugar, egg and honey in a medium bowl until combined; stir in flour mixture and nuts. Knead dough on a floured surface until smooth. Shape dough into a 25cm (10-inch) log; place on tray. Bake about 30 minutes. Cool on tray completely.

4 Reduce oven temperature to 150°C/300°F.

5 Using a serrated knife, cut log diagonally into 5mm (¼-inch) slices. Place slices, in a single layer, on ungreased oven trays. Bake about 30 minutes, turning halfway through baking time, or until biscotti are dry and crisp. Cool on wire racks.

tip Biscotti will keep in an airtight container for up to two weeks.

sugar and spice shortbread sticks

PREP + COOK TIME 45 MINUTES (+ COOLING) | MAKES 36

250g (8 ounces) butter, softened

¼ cup (55g) light brown sugar

1 teaspoon vanilla extract

2 cups (300g) plain (all-purpose) flour

⅓ cup (60g) rice flour

2 teaspoons ground fennel

½ cup (110g) demerara sugar

1 Preheat oven to 170°C/340°F. Grease and line oven trays.

2 Beat butter, brown sugar and extract in a small bowl with an electric mixer until combined; stir in sifted flours and spice, in two batches. Knead dough lightly on floured surface until smooth.

3 Divide dough into 6 equal portions; roll each portion into long 1.5cm-thick (¾ inch) lengths. Cut each length into 6 pieces. Place demerara sugar on a plate; roll each piece in sugar, place on trays.

4 Bake shortbread about 15 minutes. Cool on trays.

tip Shortbread will keep in an airtight container for up to a week.

florentine biscotti

PREP + COOK TIME 1¼ HOURS (+ COOLING & STANDING) | MAKES 60

1 cup (220g) caster (superfine) sugar

2 eggs

1 cup (150g) plain (all-purpose) flour

½ cup (75g) self-raising flour

¾ cup (60g) flaked almonds, toasted

½ cup (80g) sultanas

½ cup (100g) red glacé cherries, halved

200g (6½ ounces) dark (semi-sweet) chocolate

1 Preheat oven to 180°C/350°F. Grease and line oven trays with baking paper.

2 Whisk sugar and eggs in a medium bowl until combined; stir in sifted flours, nuts, sultanas and cherries. Shape dough into two 30cm (12-inch) logs. Place on trays; flatten slightly. Bake about 30 minutes. Cool on trays.

3 Reduce oven temperature to 140°C/275°F.

4 Using a serrated knife, slice logs diagonally into 5mm (¼-inch) slices. Place slices, in a single layer, on baking-paper-lined oven trays. Bake about 15 minutes, turning halfway through baking, or until dry and crisp. Cool on wire racks.

5 Break dark chocolate into a medium heatproof bowl. Place over a medium saucepan of simmering water (don't let water touch base of bowl); stir until chocolate is melted. Transfer chocolate to a small cup. Dip one end of biscotti into chocolate; drain excess chocolate. Place on baking-paper-lined trays. Stand at room temperature until chocolate sets.

tip Biscotti will keep in an airtight container for up to two weeks.

citrus and coconut nut bread

PREP + COOK TIME 1¾ HOURS (+ COOLING & STANDING) | MAKES 45

3 egg whites

½ cup (110g) caster (superfine) sugar

1 cup (150g) plain (all-purpose) flour

¾ cup (100g) mixed nuts

½ cup (40g) desiccated coconut

2 teaspoons each finely grated lemon, orange and lime rind

1 Preheat oven to 180°C/350°F. Grease 10cm x 20cm (4-inch x 8-inch) loaf pan.

2 Beat egg whites in a small bowl with an electric mixer until soft peaks form; gradually add sugar, beating until sugar dissolves.

3 Transfer mixture to a large bowl; stir in sifted flour, nuts, coconut and rinds. Spread mixture into pan. Bake about 30 minutes. Cool in pan.

4 Remove bread from pan, wrap in foil; stand overnight.

5 Preheat oven to 120°C/240°F.

6 Using a serrated knife, cut bread into wafer-thin slices. Place slices, in a single layer, on ungreased oven trays; bake about 45 minutes, turning halfway through baking time, or until dry and crisp. Cool bread on wire racks.

tips We used a mixture of peanuts, cashews, almond kernels and walnuts. Nut bread keeps in an airtight container for up to 1 month.

lemon poppy seed biscuits

PREP + COOK TIME 1 HOUR (+ REFRIGERATION & COOLING) | MAKES 16

You need a 7.5cm (3-inch) and a 2.5cm (1-inch) heart cutter for this recipe. You can use round cutters of similar sizes, if you prefer.

350g (11 ounces) butter, softened

½ cup (110g) caster (superfine) sugar

½ cup (80g) icing (confectioners') sugar

1 teaspoon vanilla extract

3½ cups (525g) plain (all-purpose) flour

¼ cup poppy seeds

⅔ cup (200g) lemon curd

1 Beat butter, sugars and extract in a small bowl with an electric mixer until pale and creamy. Stir in sifted flour and seeds, in two batches. Cover; refrigerate 30 minutes.

2 Preheat oven to 180°C/350°F. Grease and line oven trays with baking paper.

3 Roll dough between sheets of baking paper until 5mm (¼-inch) thick; using a large heart cutter, cut 32 hearts from dough. Place hearts, about 2.5cm (1-inch) apart, on trays. Using small heart cutter, cut centres out of 16 large hearts.

4 Bake whole hearts about 10 minutes and the remaining hearts about 8 minutes; cool on trays.

5 Spread whole hearts with curd, then top with remaining hearts.

tips We used a store-bought lemon curd in this recipe. Biscuits can be made a day ahead; they are best filled on the day of serving.

black and white cookies

PREP + COOK TIME 1 HOUR (+ COOLING & STANDING) | MAKES 16

90g (3 ounces) unsalted butter, softened

½ cup (55g) caster (superfine) sugar

1 egg

1¼ cups (185g) plain (all-purpose) flour

¼ teaspoon bicarbonate of soda (baking soda)

⅓ cup (80ml) buttermilk

1 teaspoon vanilla extract

1½ cups (240g) icing (confectioners') sugar

1 tablespoon glucose syrup

2 teaspoons lemon juice

1 tablespoon warm water

¼ cup (25g) cocoa powder

1 Preheat oven to 180°C/350°F. Line oven trays with baking paper.

2 Beat butter and caster sugar in a small bowl with an electric mixer until light and fluffy. Beat in egg until combined. Stir in sifted flour and soda, and combined buttermilk and extract.

3 Spoon 1½ tablespoons of the batter, about 5cm (2 inches) apart, onto trays. Bake about 15 minutes or until puffed and browned lightly. Transfer to a wire rack to cool.

4 Sift icing sugar into a small bowl; stir in glucose, juice and the water until smooth. Transfer half the icing to another small bowl; stir in sifted cocoa, adding a little water if necessary.

5 Turn cookies flat-side up; spread white icing over one half of each cookie. Spread chocolate icing over remaining half. Stand on a wire rack until set.

tips Glucose syrup is often quite difficult to measure as it is very thick and sticks to everything. To make it easier, warm the jar of glucose syrup in a bowl of hot water before spooning out the required amount. Lightly oiling the spoon, or heating the spoon under hot water, and drying, will also help you to spoon the syrup out of the jar.
The biscuits will keep in an airtight container for up to three days.

lime and vanilla madeleines

PREP + COOK TIME 45 MINUTES | MAKES 20

2 eggs

2 tablespoons caster (superfine) sugar

2 tablespoons icing (confectioners') sugar

2 vanilla beans

75g (2½ ounces) butter

¼ cup (35g) self-raising flour

¼ cup (35g) plain (all-purpose) flour

1 teaspoon finely grated lime rind

1 tablespoon lime juice

1 tablespoon hot water

2 tablespoons icing (confectioners') sugar, extra

1 Preheat oven to 200°C/400°F. Grease two standard 12-hole (1½-tablespoons/30ml) madeleine pans.

2 Place eggs and sugars in a small bowl. Split vanilla beans lengthways; scrape seeds into bowl with eggs. Beat with an electric mixer until thick and creamy.

3 Meanwhile, melt butter. Sift flours twice, then sift flours over egg mixture; pour combined melted butter, rind, juice and the water down side of bowl, then fold ingredients together.

4 Drop rounded tablespoons of mixture into pan holes. Bake madeleines about 10 minutes. Tap hot pan firmly on bench to release madeleines, then turn immediately onto baking-paper-covered wire racks to cool. Serve dusted with extra sifted icing sugar.

tip Madeleines should be eaten soon after baking.

hazelnut crescents

PREP + COOK TIME 1 HOUR (+ REFRIGERATION & COOLING) | MAKES 30

250g (8 ounces) butter, softened

1 egg

1 vanilla bean

2 cups (300g) plain (all-purpose) flour

1 cup (160g) icing (confectioner's) sugar

¾ cup (75g) ground hazelnuts

1 teaspoon finely grated orange rind

1 teaspoon ground cinnamon

1 cup (160g) icing (confectioner's) sugar, extra

1 Place butter and egg in a medium bowl. Split vanilla bean lengthways; scrape seeds into butter mixture. Beat with an electric mixer until combined. Stir in sifted flour and icing sugar, ground hazelnuts, rind and cinnamon. Wrap dough in plastic wrap; refrigerate 2 hours.

2 Preheat oven to 160°C/325°F.

3 Divide dough into 3 portions; split each portion evenly into 10 pieces. Roll each piece into a small crescent shape.

4 Place crescents, about 5cm (2 inches) apart, on baking-paper-lined trays. Bake crescents about 15 minutes. Transfer to a wire rack to cool.

5 Place extra icing sugar in a medium bowl, toss biscuits, one at a time, in sugar to coat generously.

tip Crescents will keep in an airtight container for up to 1 week.

DESSERTS

mini marmalade queen of puddings

PREP + COOK TIME 40 MINUTES (+ STANDING) | MAKES 8

2 teaspoons caster (superfine) sugar

1 cup (70g) stale breadcrumbs

1 teaspoon vanilla extract

2 teaspoons finely grated orange rind

1¼ cups (310ml) milk

30g (1 ounce) butter

2 eggs, separated

⅓ cup (115g) orange marmalade

½ cup (110g) caster (superfine) sugar, extra

1 Preheat oven to 180°C/350°F. Grease eight ⅓-cup (80ml) ovenproof espresso cups or dishes; place on an oven tray.

2 Combine sugar, breadcrumbs, extract and rind in a medium heatproof bowl. Heat milk and butter in a small saucepan until almost boiling; pour over breadcrumb mixture, stand 10 minutes. Stir egg yolks into breadcrumb mixture.

3 Divide rounded tablespoons of breadcrumb mixture into cups; level tops. Bake 20 minutes.

4 Meanwhile, warm marmalade. Carefully spread tops of hot puddings with warmed marmalade.

5 While puddings are baking, beat egg whites and extra sugar in a small bowl with an electric mixer until sugar is dissolved. Spoon meringue in peaks on tops of puddings. Bake about 5 minutes or until meringue is browned lightly.

tips You can use lemon, lime or blood orange marmalade or your favourite jam instead of orange marmalade.

white chocolate cream with poached peaches

PREP + COOK TIME 35 MINUTES (+ COOLING & REFRIGERATION) | SERVES 6

1 vanilla bean

125g (8 ounces) white chocolate

300ml (½ pint) pouring cream

2 tablespoons caster (superfine) sugar

1½ teaspoons powdered gelatine

1 tablespoon boiling water

½ cup (140g) greek-style yogurt

POACHED PEACHES

3 medium yellow peaches (300g)

2 cups (500ml) water

1 cup (220g) caster (superfine) sugar

1 cinnamon stick

1 Split vanilla bean lengthways. Break chocolate into a small saucepan; add cream, sugar and vanilla bean, stir over low heat until smooth. Cool 5 minutes.
2 Sprinkle gelatine over the boiling water in a small heatproof bowl. Stand bowl in a small saucepan of simmering water; stir until gelatine dissolves. Stir gelatine mixture into cream mixture. Cool 15 minutes. Discard vanilla bean.
3 Add yogurt to cream mixture; whisk to combine. Pour mixture into six 1½-cup (375ml) glasses. Cover loosely with plastic wrap; refrigerate 4 hours or overnight until set.
4 Make poached peaches.
5 Serve chocolate cream topped with peach halves and a little of the reserved syrup.

POACHED PEACHES Halve peaches; discard seeds. Stir the water, sugar and cinnamon in a small saucepan over medium heat, without boiling, until sugar dissolves. Bring to the boil. Reduce heat, add peaches; simmer, uncovered, about 5 minutes or until peaches are just tender. Cool peaches in syrup. Discard cinnamon stick. Remove peaches; discard skins. Reserve ½ cup syrup (keep remaining liquid for another use).

tips Choose freestone peaches as it will be easier to remove the seeds. Keep any leftover poaching liquid to poach other fruit, or reduce to a syrup by simmering gently, and pour over ice-cream.

fruit salad with middle-eastern flavours

PREP + COOK TIME 30 MINUTES | SERVES 6

3 medium navel oranges (720g)

10 cardamom pods

¾ cup (165g) caster sugar

1½ cups (375ml) water

1 vanilla bean, split lengthways, seeds scraped

1 large carrot (180g), cut into matchsticks

1 pomegranate (450g)

3 medium blood oranges (720g)

5 medium peaches (750g), halved, seeds removed, cut into wedges

½ cup (125ml) fresh orange juice

⅓ cup (80ml) fresh lemon juice

1 Using a vegetable peeler, peel rind from one navel orange. Place rind, cardamom, sugar, the water, vanilla bean and seeds, in a small pan; stir over low heat until sugar dissolves.

2 Add carrot; increase heat to medium; cook about 20 minutes or until syrup is thick and carrot is translucent. Using a fork, transfer candied carrot to a small bowl. Transfer unstrained syrup to large bowl.

3 Remove seeds from pomegranate; reserve seeds. Using a small sharp knife, remove rind and pith from navel and blood oranges, following the curve of the fruit. Cut oranges into 5mm (¼-inch) thick rounds; add to the syrup with pomegranate seeds and peaches. Add juices to bowl; stir to combine.

4 Stir half the candied carrot into fruit salad; divide fruit salad into small bowls, top with remaining candied carrot.

tips You will need about 2 extra navel oranges and 2 lemons for the juice in this recipe. The easiest way to remove seeds from a pomegranate is to cut it in half, then release the seeds in a large bowl of water. This way you won't get splattered with juice and the white pith will float.

poached peaches in vanilla syrup

PREP + COOK TIME 30 MINUTES (+ COOLING & REFRIGERATION) | SERVES 8

1.5kg (3 pounds) white peaches

3 cups (660g) caster (superfine) sugar

1.5 litres (6 cups) water

1 vanilla bean

1 Make small incisions at the base of each peach.

2 Combine sugar and the water in a large saucepan. Using a sharp knife, split vanilla bean and scrape seeds into saucepan, add bean. Cook, stirring, over medium heat, until sugar has dissolved. Increase heat to high; bring to the boil.

3 Add fruit; return to the boil. Immediately reduce heat to a very gentle simmer; place a small plate over fruit to weigh them down in the liquid. Poach 5 minutes or until just tender.

4 Remove plate; remove fruit with a slotted spoon. (Once the fruit has cooled, you can slip off the skins, if you like, but it's not necessary to do so.)

5 Return syrup to medium heat; simmer about 20 minutes or until syrup is reduced to 4 cups. Cool completely before pouring over fruit. Refrigerate, covered, 2-3 days before eating.

tips These peaches will keep for 1 week stored in an airtight container in the fridge. After 2 days, the liquid will increase by half, and the flavours will intensify. Make sure the fruit is covered in the poaching liquid. Keep any leftover poaching liquid to poach other fruit, or reduce to a syrup by simmering gently, and pour over ice-cream. Choose freestone peaches, as it will be easier to remove the seeds.

serving suggestion Vanilla ice-cream and amaretti biscuits.

roasted peaches with vanilla and honey

PREP + COOK TIME 40 MINUTES | SERVES 4

4 large white peaches (880g)

1 vanilla bean

2 tablespoons honey

1 tablespoon lemon juice

30g (1 ounce) butter

1 Preheat oven to 200°C/400°F.

2 Halve peaches; remove and discard seeds. Place peaches, cut-side, up in a single layer, in a shallow baking dish.

3 Using a sharp knife, split vanilla bean and scrape seeds into a small saucepan, add bean. Add honey and juice to pan; cook over low heat until liquid is of a pourable consistency. Pour over peaches. Chop butter; scatter over fruit. Roast peaches, uncovered, about 30 minutes, basting regularly, or until tender.

tip Choose freestone peaches as it will be easier to remove the seeds. You can peel the peaches before roasting if you prefer.

serving suggestion Serve peaches warm with crème fraîche or mascarpone.

boca negra

PREP + COOK TIME 50 MINUTES (+ REFRIGERATION) | SERVES 20

½ cup (125ml) bourbon

1½ cups (330g) caster (superfine) sugar

400g (12½ ounces) dark (semi-sweet) chocolate, chopped finely

250g (8 ounces) unsalted butter, chopped coarsely

5 eggs

1 tablespoon dutch cocoa

1¾ cup (375ml) double (thick) cream

1 Preheat oven to 180°C/350°F. Grease deep 22cm (9-inch) round cake pan; line base and side with baking paper.

2 Stir bourbon and sugar in a small saucepan over medium heat, without boiling, until sugar dissolves. Blend or process chocolate and bourbon mixture until smooth. With motor operating, add butter, piece by piece, processing until combined. Add eggs, one at a time, processing until combined between additions. Pour mixture into pan.

3 Place pan in a large baking dish. Pour enough boiling water into baking dish to come halfway up side of pan. Bake about 30 minutes or until edge is set (centre will still be a little soft). Remove pan from dish; cool 10 minutes. Cover; refrigerate 4 hours or overnight until set.

4 Carefully turn cake out of pan onto serving plate; dust lightly with cocoa. Serve with double cream.

tip Boca negra, Spanish for 'black mouth', is a silky, fudgy, moist chocolate cake, and is so named as it will turn your mouth black with chocolate after just one bite.

peach and nectarine trifle

PREP + COOK TIME 1 HOUR (+ COOLING & REFRIGERATION) | SERVES 8

3 eggs, separated

½ cup (110g) caster (superfine) sugar

350g (11 ounces) mascarpone cheese, softened

2 tablespoons orange-flavoured liqueur

250g (8 ounces) sponge finger biscuits (savoiardi)

POACHED PEACHES AND NECTARINES

750g (1½ pounds) yellow peaches

750g (1½ pounds) yellow nectarines

3 cups (660g) caster (superfine) sugar

1.5 litres (6 cups) water

1 vanilla bean, split, seeds scraped

large strips rind from 1 orange

1 Make poached peaches and nectarines.

2 Beat sugar and egg yolks in a small bowl with an electric mixer about 5 minutes or until pale and tripled in volume. Fold through mascarpone.

3 Beat egg whites in another small bowl until soft peaks form. Fold gently through yolk mixture until smooth.

4 Slip skins off fruit. Halve fruit; discard seeds. Cut fruit into thin wedges. Stir liqueur through reserved poaching liquid.

5 Cover bases of eight 1-cup (250ml) serving glasses with a layer of mascarpone mixture.

6 Working in batches, dip enough biscuits into poaching liquid to cover top of mascarpone mixture (break biscuits to fit, if necessary); top with another layer of mascarpone mixture, then top with fruit.

7 Cover with plastic wrap; refrigerate until ready to serve.

POACHED PEACHES AND NECTARINES Make small cuts into the base of each fruit. Combine sugar, the water, vanilla seeds and bean, and orange rind in a large saucepan. Cook on medium heat, stirring, until sugar has dissolved. Bring to the boil, add fruit; return to the boil. Immediately reduce heat to a very gentle simmer; place a small plate over fruit to weigh them down in the liquid. Poach fruit 5 minutes or until just tender. Remove plate; remove fruit with a slotted spoon. Discard rind. Measure 2 cups of poaching liquid (keep remaining liquid for another use); cool reserved liquid and fruit separately.

tips This recipe must be eaten on the day it is made. When beating the egg whites, make sure the bowl and beaters and clean and dry. We used Cointreau, but you can use your favourite orange- or citrus-flavoured liqueur. The poached fruit will keep for 2-3 days, covered, in the refrigerator but the fruit will generate a lot of syrup. Choose freestone peaches and nectarines as it will be easier to remove the seeds. Keep any leftover poaching liquid to poach other fruit, or reduce to a syrup by simmering gently, and pour over ice-cream.

chocolate and cinnamon affogato shots

PREP + COOK TIME 30 MINUTES | SERVES 4

1 tablespoon instant espresso coffee granules

2 tablespoons caster (superfine) sugar

1 cinnamon stick

¼ cup (60ml) water

2 tablespoons coffee-flavoured liqueur

50g (1½ ounces) dark (semi-sweet) chocolate, grated finely

4 small scoops vanilla or chocolate ice-cream

1 Stir coffee, sugar, cinnamon and the water in a small saucepan over medium heat, without boiling, until coffee and sugar dissolve. Bring to the boil. Remove from heat; stand, covered, 10 minutes. Discard cinnamon stick.

2 Return coffee syrup to the boil. Remove from heat; stir in liqueur and half the grated chocolate.

3 Scoop ice-cream into four ½-cup (125ml) serving glasses; sprinkle with remaining chocolate. Pour hot coffee syrup over ice-cream. Serve coffee shots immediately.

tip We used Tia Maria for this recipe, but you can use your favourite coffee-flavoured liqueur.

strawberry tiramisu

PREP + COOK TIME 40 MINUTES (+ REFRIGERATION) | SERVES 6

½ cup (125ml) pouring cream

½ cup (125g) mascarpone cheese

⅓ cup (75g) caster (superfine) sugar

3 egg yolks

6 sponge finger biscuits (savoiardi) (130g)

STRAWBERRY SAUCE

200g (6½ ounces) strawberries

1 tablespoon lemon juice

1 tablespoon icing (confectioners') sugar

1 tablespoon water, approximately

1 Make strawberry sauce.

2 Beat cream, mascarpone and 1 tablespoon of the sugar in a small bowl with an electric mixer until soft peaks form. Beat egg yolks and remaining sugar in another small bowl with an electric mixer until thick and creamy. Fold egg yolk mixture into mascarpone mixture.

3 Cut biscuits into half or thirds (depending on the size of the base of your glasses). Pour ¾ cup of strawberry sauce into a small bowl; dip biscuits into sauce. Place soaked biscuits into bases of six ¾-cup (180ml) small wine glasses. Divide mascarpone mixture into glasses. Cover; refrigerate 1 hour. Refrigerate remaining strawberry sauce.

4 Just before serving, pour remaining strawberry sauce into each glass.

STRAWBERRY SAUCE Chop strawberries coarsely. Blend or process strawberries until smooth. Strain puree into a small jug; discard seeds. Stir juice, sugar and enough of the water into puree to make 1 cup of sauce.

sweet peach and thyme pizza

PREP + COOK TIME 20 MINUTES (+ STANDING) | SERVES 6

1¼ cups (185g) plain (all-purpose) flour

1 tablespoon caster (superfine) sugar

1 teaspoon dried instant yeast

pinch salt

½ cup (125ml) warm water

1 tablespoon olive oil

1 tablespoon fresh thyme sprigs

2 large yellow peaches (440g)

2 tablespoons demerara sugar

1 Combine flour, caster sugar, yeast and salt in a large bowl. Stir in the water and olive oil. Turn dough onto a lightly floured surface; knead lightly (adding a little more flour if necessary) until dough forms a smooth, soft ball. Place in a lightly oiled clean bowl; cover with a tea towel. Stand dough in a warm, draft-free place for about 1 hour or until doubled in size.

2 Preheat oven to 240°C/475°F. Grease large oven tray.

3 Punch air out of dough. Divide dough equally in half. Roll each half thinly on a floured surface into a 30cm (12-inch) oval. Place on trays; sprinkle over half the thyme.

4 Halve peaches; discard seeds. Thinly slice peaches; arrange on dough. Sprinkle over demerara sugar. Bake about 10 minutes until golden and base is crisp. Serve immediately sprinkled with remaining thyme.

tip Choose freestone peaches as it will be easier to remove the seeds.

spiced plum and apple crumble

PREP + COOK TIME 1 HOUR | SERVES 6

500g (1 pound) apples

¾ cup (165g) caster (superfine) sugar

2 tablespoons water

700g (1½ pounds) red-fleshed plums

125g (4 ounces) cold unsalted butter

1 cup (150g) plain (all-purpose) flour

½ cup (110g) firmly packed light brown sugar

1 teaspoon mixed spice

¼ cup (20g) flaked almonds

1 Preheat oven to 200°C/400°F.

2 Peel, core and cut apples into chunks. Put in a large saucepan with caster sugar and the water; cook, stirring, over medium heat, until sugar dissolves. Cover; cook 10 minutes or until apple is just tender.

3 Quarter plums, discard seeds; stir into apples in pan. Cook, covered, about 5 minutes or until plums are soft but still hold their shape.

4 Remove fruit from syrup with a slotted spoon; transfer to a 1.25-litre (5-cup) ovenproof dish. Reserve the syrup.

5 Chop butter finely. Combine flour, brown sugar and mixed spice in a large bowl. Rub butter into mixture with fingertips until mixture resembles breadcrumbs and starts to clump together. Fold through almonds; sprinkle over fruit.

6 Bake 30 minutes or until golden and bubbling. Serve crumble warm, drizzled with double cream and reserved syrup if you like.

tips We used pink lady apples in this recipe, as they tend to hold their shape well. You can keep and use the syrup at a later date to serve over ice-cream and fresh berries.

serving suggestion Double (thick) cream or vanilla ice-cream.

COOKING TECHNIQUES

To rub in butter Chop the cold butter into cubes; use your fingertips (the coolest part of your hands) to squash the butter through the flour. Do this quickly to keep the butter cold.

To blind bake pastry, cover the pastry with baking paper; fill with uncooked rice or dried beans. Cook the pastry for 10 minutes, then remove the paper and rice; cook it a further 10 minutes (or as indicated by the recipe) or until the pastry is golden.

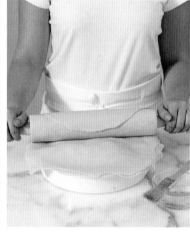

To cover a pie top with pastry, brush the pastry edge with a little water. Roll the pastry about 5cm larger than the top of the dish. Gently roll the pastry around the rolling pin; unroll it over the filling to completely cover the top of the pie dish.

To trim the pastry, hold the pie dish flat on the palm of one hand, then use a sharp knife to make a downward cutting action, and trim away the excess pastry at a 45° angle.

To make small chocolate curls, have a large, unbroken block of chocolate at room temperature. Using a sharp vegetable peeler, drag the peeler down the length of the chocolate along the side to make small curls.

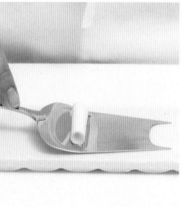

To make large chocolate curls, gently rub the palm of your hand over the back of a block of chocolate for about a minute to slightly warm it. Drag a sharp cheese slicer down the chocolate to make curls.

To melt chocolate, place roughly chopped chocolate into a heatproof bowl over a pan of barely simmering water. The water mustn't touch the base of the bowl. Stir chocolate until smooth, and remove from the pan as soon as it's melted.

To make toffee (1), stir sugar and the water over a high heat, without boiling, until the sugar dissolves. Use a pastry brush dipped in water to brush any sugar grains from the side of the pan back into the syrup.

To toast coconut, stir the coconut over a low heat in a dry frying pan until golden brown. Remove the coconut immediately from the pan to stop it from burning.

Making choux pastry While the pan is still over the heat, add the flour all at once. Use a wooden spoon to briskly beat the ingredients over the heat until the mixture forms a ball and pulls away from the side and the base of the pan.

To split a cake into even layers, use skewers as a guide for the knife as you split the cake. For large cakes, push long skewers through the cake; for small cakes, use toothpicks to mark the layer. Use a sharp serrated knife to split the cake. Cut the cake barely above the skewers.

To cover the side of a cake, cover the side with frosting, butter cream or icing. Spread coconut (or whatever covering is to be used) in a large flat pan and, holding the cake like a wheel, roll it in the frosting until it is evenly covered.

To make toffee (2), once the sugar has come to the boil, stop stirring and boil the mixture until the bubbles are large and thick, and the syrup is a golden amber colour (or until the required temperature is reached on a digital or sugar thermometer).

To make caramel hazelnuts (1) (dobos torte, page 32), first place two jars on top of a piece of baking paper, then tie string between the jars (the string must be far enough off the bench so the toffee can drip unimpeded – see step 2, right). Bend the top of 12 toothpicks over, then push the skinned nuts onto the tips. Boil the sugar syrup until it's a deep golden colour: remove from the heat and dip a nut into the toffee.

To make caramel hazelnuts (2), hook the broken end of the toothpick over the string; repeat with the remaining nuts, one at a time, making sure the nuts don't touch each other as you hang them. Once the toffee has hardened, place on top of the torte. It is best not to make toffee if the weather is humid, as humidity will make the toffee soft and it will not hold its shape.

To use a sugar thermometer, put it in a small saucepan of cold water, bring it to the boil. When the syrup begins to boil, put the thermometer into the syrup. Leave it in the syrup until the temperature required is reached, then return it to the pan of boiling water; turn the heat off, cool. Wash any excess caramel from the thermometer, then dry and store carefully.

113

GLOSSARY

ALLSPICE also known as pimento or jamaican pepper; available whole or ground. Tastes like a blend of clove, cinnamon and nutmeg - all spices.

BAKING PAPER also parchment paper or baking parchment; a silicone-coated paper that is primarily used for lining baking pans and oven trays so cakes and biscuits won't stick, making removal easy.

BLUEBERRIES a dark navy-blue to blue-black coloured round berry covered in a fine, white powder or 'bloom'. Blueberries are very perishable, so keep them refrigerated and use as soon as possible.

BICARBONATE OF SODA also known as baking soda or carb soda. A raising agent used in baking.

BUTTER unless otherwise indicated, butter should be at room temperature before using. An exception to this is when making pastry, where the butter should be cold. 125g is equal to one stick (4 ounces) of butter.

Unsalted butter, often called 'sweet' butter, simply has no added salt. It is mainly used in baking, and if the recipe calls for unsalted butter, then it should not be substituted.

BUTTERMILK originally the term given to the slightly sour liquid left after butter was churned from cream, today it is made similarly to yogurt. Sold alongside all fresh milk products in supermarkets. Despite its name, it is low in fat.

CACHOUS also known as dragées; minuscule metallic-looking-but-edible confectionery balls; available in silver, gold or various colours.

CARDAMOM a spice native to India; can be purchased in pod, seed or ground form. It has a distinctive aromatic and sweetly rich flavour, and is one of the world's most expensive spices.

CHEESE

cream commonly known as Philly or Philadelphia, a soft cow's-milk cheese with a high fat content.

mascarpone an Italian fresh cultured-cream product made similarly to yogurt. Whiteish to creamy yellow in colour, with a buttery-rich, luscious, soft and creamy texture.

ricotta the name for this soft, white, cow's-milk cheese roughly translates as 'cooked again'. It's made from whey, a by-product of other cheese-making, to which fresh milk and acid are added. Ricotta is a sweet, moist cheese with a slightly grainy texture.

CHERRIES, GLACÉ also called candied cherries; cherries are boiled in a heavy sugar syrup.

CHOCOLATE

dark (semi-sweet) also called luxury chocolate; made of a high percentage of cocoa liquor and cocoa butter, and a little added sugar.

choc Bits also known as chocolate chips and chocolate morsels; available in milk, white and dark.

melts small discs of compounded milk, white or dark chocolate ideal for melting and moulding.

milk the most popular eating chocolate, mild and very sweet; similar to dark with the difference being the addition of milk solids.

white contains no cocoa solids but derives its sweet flavour from cocoa butter. Is very sensitive to heat, so watch carefully when melting.

CINNAMON dried inner bark of the shoots of the cinnamon tree; available in stick (quill) or ground form.

CLOVES dried flower buds of a tropical tree; can be used whole or in ground form. Has a distinctively pungent and 'spicy' scent and flavour.

COCOA POWDER also known as cocoa; dried, unsweetened, roasted then ground cocoa beans (cacao seeds).

dutch cocoa is treated with an alkali to neutralize its acids. It has a dark reddish-brown colour, mild flavour, and is easy to dissolve in liquids. It is available in specialist food stores and delicatessens.

COCONUT

cream obtained from the first pressing of the coconut flesh alone, without the addition of water.

desiccated concentrated, dried, finely shredded, unsweetened coconut flesh. Is a finer cut than shredded.

extract synthetically produced from flavouring, oil and alcohol.

flaked dried flaked coconut flesh.

fresh to open a fresh coconut, pierce one of the eyes then roast coconut briefly in a very hot oven only until cracks appear in the shell. Cool, then hit the coconut to break apart.

milk not the juice found inside the fruit (which is coconut water), but the diluted liquid pressed from the white meat of a mature coconut. After the liquid settles, the cream and 'milk' (thin white fluid) separate naturally.

shredded thin strips of dried coconut.

To toast coconut, stir coconut in a medium frying pan, over low heat, about 3 minutes or until golden. Remove from the pan immediately to prevent over-browning or burning.

CORNFLOUR (cornstarch) available made from 100% corn (maize) or wheat; used as a thickening agent.

CREAM

pouring also called single, fresh or pure cream. It has no additives and a minimum fat content of 35%.

thick (double) a dolloping cream with a minimum fat content of 45%.

thickened (heavy) a whipping cream containing a thickener; has a minimum fat content of 35%.

CUSTARD POWDER instant mixture used to make pouring custard; similar to North American instant vanilla pudding mixes.

ESSENCE/EXTRACT an essence is either a distilled concentration of a food quality or an artificial creation of it. Coconut and almond essences are synthetically produced. An extract is made by extracting the flavour from a food product. In the case of vanilla, pods are soaked, usually in alcohol, to capture the authentic flavour. Essences and extracts keep indefinitely if stored in a cool dark place.

EGGS we use large eggs in this book with a average weight of 60g. Unless otherwise indicated, when baking, eggs, either whole or separated, should be at room temperature before using. Some recipes in this book may call for raw or barely cooked eggs; exercise caution if there is a salmonella problem in your area. The risk is greater for those who are pregnant, elderly or very young, and those with impaired immune systems.

FIGS vary in skin and flesh colour according to type not ripeness. When ripe, figs should be unblemished and bursting with flesh; nectar beads at the base indicate when a fig is at its best. Also available glacéd (candied), dried or canned in sugar syrup; these are usually sold at health-food stores, Middle-Eastern food shops, specialty cheese shops and delicatessens.

FLOUR
baker's also known as bread-mix and gluten-enriched flour. Produced from a variety of wheat that has a high gluten (protein) content and is best suited for pizza and bread making. It is available from health food stores and supermarkets.
plain (all-purpose) unbleached wheat flour, is the best for baking: the gluten content ensures a strong dough, which produces a light result.
self-raising (self-rising) plain flour that has been sifted with baking powder in the proportion of 1 cup flour to 2 teaspoons baking powder.

FOOD COLOURING dyes used to change the colour of various foods; they are edible and do not change the taste to a noticeable extent.

GELATINE we use powdered gelatine in our recipes. It is also available in sheet form, known as leaf gelatine. If using gelatine leaves , three teaspoons of powdered gelatine (8g or one sachet) roughly equals four gelatine leaves.

GHEE a type of clarified butter that is most frequently used in Indian cooking; milk solids are cooked until they are a golden brown colour (whereas in clarified butter they are not). This imparts a nutty flavour and sweet aroma; ghee can be heated to a high temperature without burning.

GINGER
glacé fresh ginger root preserved in sugar syrup; crystallised ginger can be substituted if rinsed with warm water and dried before using.
ground also called powdered ginger; used as a flavouring but cannot be substituted for fresh ginger.

GLUCOSE SYRUP also known as liquid glucose, made from wheat starch; used in jam and confectionery making. Available at health food stores and supermarkets.

GOLDEN SYRUP a by-product of refined sugarcane; pure maple syrup or honey can be substituted.

HAZELNUTS, GROUND hazelnuts are ground into a coarse or fine powder; also known as hazelnut meal (see also under 'nuts').

JAM also known as preserve or conserve; most often made from fruit.

LIQUEUR we used the following, but use your favourite brand if you prefer.
cherry-flavoured kirsch.
chocolate-flavoured creme de cacao.
citrus-flavoured cointreau.
coconut-flavoured malibu.
coffee-flavoured kahlua or tia maria.
hazelnut-flavoured frangelico.
orange-flavoured curacao or grand marnier (based on cognac-brandy).
raspberry-flavoured framboise.

LYCHEE a small fruit from China with a hard shell and sweet, juicy flesh. The white flesh has a gelatinous texture and musky, perfumed taste. Discard the rough skin and seed before using.

MALTED MILK POWDER a combination of wheat flour, malt flour and milk, which is evaporated to give the powder its fine appearance and to make it easily absorbable in liquids.

MARZIPAN made from ground almonds, sugar and glucose. Similar to almond paste but is not as strong in flavour; is finer in consistency and more pliable. Cheaper brands often use ground apricot kernels and sugar.

MIXED SPICE a blend of ground spices usually consisting of allspice, cinnamon and nutmeg.

NUTMEG a strong and pungent spice from the dried nut of a native Indonesian evergreen tree. Usually found ground, the flavour is more intense when freshly grated from the whole nut (available from spice shops).

NUTS
almonds flat, pointy-ended nut with a pitted brown shell enclosing a creamy white kernel that is covered by a brown skin. *Blanched almonds* are whole nuts that have had the brown skins removed. *Flaked almonds* are paper-thin slices. *Ground almonds* are also known as almond meal.
cashew a kidney-shaped nut that grows out from the bottom of the cashew apple. They have a sweet, buttery flavour and a high fat content, so store, tightly wrapped, in the refrigerator to slow rancidity.
hazelnut also known as filberts; plump, grape-sized, rich, sweet nut having a brown inedible skin that is removed by rubbing heated nuts

together vigorously in a tea towel.

macadamia a rich, buttery nut; should be stored in the refrigerator because of its high oil content.

pecans native to the United States and now grown in Australia; a buttery-rich, golden-brown nut.

pine nuts also known as pignoli; not, in fact, a nut, but a small, cream-coloured kernel from pine cones.

pistachio pale green, delicately sweet flavoured, crunchy nut inside hard off-white shells. To peel nuts, soak shelled nuts in boiling water for about 5 minutes; drain, then pat dry with absorbent paper towel. Rub skins with a clean tea towel to remove.

walnut the nuts have a smooth outer green husk that is removed when the ripe nuts are harvested and sold. The kernel is ridged and oval and formed in two distinct halves.

To toast nuts, place shelled, peeled nuts, in a single layer, in a small dry frying pan; cook over low heat, stirring frequently, until nuts are fragrant and just changed in colour. Remove from pan immediately to avoid burning.

PASSIONFRUIT also known as granadilla; a small tropical fruit that is native to Brazil. Comprised of a tough outer skin surrounding edible black sweet-sour seeds and pulp.

PASTRY

fillo is unique in that no margarine or fat is added to the dough. The dough is very elastic in texture and not rolled like other pastries, but stretched to the desired thickness. This gives it its unique, delicate, tissue-thin sheets. It is best brushed with melted margarine or butter before baking.

puff a crisp, light pastry; layers of dough and shortening are folded and rolled many times making many layers. When baked, it becomes a high, crisp, flaky pastry. Butter puff pastry uses butter for the shortening, whereas puff pastry uses a blend of vegetable and animal fats.

sheets packaged ready-rolled sheets of frozen puff and shortcrust pastry, available from supermarkets.

shortcrust a tender, crunchy, melt-in-the-mouth buttery pastry. Once baked, it is a light, crumbly, easily broken short pastry.

PEANUT BRITTLE peanuts are coated in a hard toffee coating; available from confectionery stores and most major supermarkets.

PURE MAPLE SYRUP a thin syrup distilled from the sap of the maple tree. Maple-flavoured syrup or pancake syrup are not adequate substitutes for the real thing.

RAISINS dried sweet grapes.

RASPBERRIES known as the 'King of the Berries' about 1.5-2cm long, cylinder-shaped, with a deep-red colouring and a sweet flavour. Also available black or yellow in colour. Are actually a collection of tiny fruits, each with its own seed covered in red skin and flesh, which form a cluster around a small stem. When harvested the cluster comes away from the stem leaving a hollow in the centre. These very fragile berries spoil rapidly, so check for mildew when buying. Also available frozen.

RHUBARB a plant with long, green-red stalks; becomes sweet and edible when cooked. The stalks are the only edible portion of the plant – the leaves contain a toxic substance.

ROSEWATER extract made from crushed rose petals; used for its aromatic quality in many sweetmeats and desserts. Don't confuse with rose essence, which is more concentrated.

SULTANAS dried grapes, also known as golden raisins.

SUGAR

caster (superfine) also called finely granulated table sugar.

brown a finely granulated, very soft sugar retaining molasses for its characteristic colour and flavour.

dark brown a moist, dark brown sugar with a rich, distinctive, full flavour coming from natural molasses syrup.

demerara this granulated, golden coloured sugar has a distinctive rich flavour; often used to sweeten coffee.

icing (confectioners') also known as powdered sugar; granulated sugar crushed together with a little added cornflour (cornstarch).

pearl also called nib or hail sugar; a product of refined white sugar, it is very coarse, hard, opaque white, and doesn't melt during baking. Available from specialist food stores.

pure icing (confectioners') also known as powdered sugar, but has no added cornflour (cornstarch).

raw natural brown granulated sugar.

white (granulated) also called crystal sugar; coarse, granulated table sugar.

TREACLE a concentrated, refined sugar syrup with a distinctive flavour and dark black colour.

TURKISH DELIGHT an extremely popular Middle-Eastern sweet. A mixture of syrup and cornflour is boiled with either honey or fruit juice, and then flavoured with rosewater or peppermint. Once set, the mixture is rolled in icing sugar. Turkish delight is available in confectionery shops and most major supermarkets.

VANILLA

bean dried, long, thin pod; the tiny black seeds inside are used to impart a luscious vanilla flavour in baking.

extract obtained from vanilla beans infused in water; a non-alcoholic version of essence. Vanilla essence, or imitation vanilla extract, is not a satisfactory substitute.

paste made from vanilla pods and contains real vanilla seeds. It is highly concentrated and 1 teaspoon of paste replaces a whole vanilla pod.

INDEX

Published in 2013 by ACP Books, Sydney

ACP Books are published by ACP Magazines Limited

a division of Nine Entertainment Co.

54 Park St, Sydney

GPO Box 4088, Sydney, NSW 2001.

phone (02) 9282 8618; fax (02) 9126 3702

acpbooks@acpmagazines.com.au; www.acpbooks.com.au

ACP BOOKS

Publishing Director, ACP Magazines - Gerry Reynolds

Publisher - Sally Wright

Editorial and Food Director - Pamela Clark

Creative Director - Hieu Chi Nguyen

Published and Distributed in the United Kingdom by Octopus Publishing Group

Endeavour House

189 Shaftesbury Avenue

London WC2H 8JY

United Kingdom

phone (+44)(0)207 632 5400; fax (+44)(0)207 632 5405

info@octopus-publishing.co.uk;

www.octopusbooks.co.uk

Printed by Toppan Printing Co., China

ational foreign language rights, Brian Cearnes, ACP Books bcearnes@acpmagazines.com.au

A catalogue record for this book is available from the British Library.

ISBN: 978-174245-307-1 (pbk.)

© ACP Magazines Ltd 2013

ABN 18 053 273 546

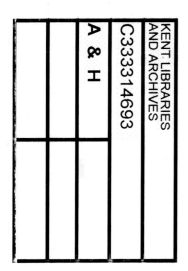